THE FRENCH COOK

SOUPS & STEWS

HOLLY HERRICK

Photographs by Chia Chong

GIBBS SMITH
TO ENRICH AND INSPIRE HUMANKIND

To all French chefs everywhere and to those who embrace the soul-enriching value of a delicious soup and its simple yet nuanced preparation. *Merci a vous!* The world and her soups and stews would surely not be nearly as delicious without you.

First Edition
18 17 16 15 14   5 4 3 2 1

Text © 2014 Holly Herrick
Photographs © 2014 Chia Chong

Published by
Gibbs Smith
P.O. Box 667
Layton, Utah 84041

1.800.835.4993 orders
www.gibbs-smith.com

Design by Sheryl Dickert
Page production by Melissa Dymock
Food and prop styling by Libbie Summers

Printed and bound in China

Gibbs Smith books are printed on either recycled, 100% post-consumer waste, FSC-certified papers or on paper produced from sustainable PEFC-certified forest/controlled wood source. Learn more at www.pefc.org.

Library of Congress Cataloging-in-Publication Data

Herrick, Holly.
 The French cook. Soups & stews / Holly Herrick ; photographs by Chia Chong. — First edition.
 pages cm
 Includes index.
 ISBN 978-1-4236-3576-5
 1. Soups. 2. Stews. 3. Cooking, French. I. Title.
 II. Title: Soups & stews.
 TX757.H477 2014
 641.81'3—dc23
 2014003158

Other books in The French Cook series:

Cream Puffs & Eclairs

Sauces

Soufflés

"Bouillabaisse is only good because [it is] cooked by the French, who, if they cared to try, could produce an excellent and nutritious substitute out of cigar stumps and empty match boxes."

–Norman Douglas, 1868-1952, from *Siren Land*

CONTENTS

INTRODUCTION

It sounds counterintuitive, but when cooking, the simpler something is to prepare, the more difficult it is to make it delicious, or even perfect.

No singular food preparation holds more firmly to this truth than making soups or stews, particularly if they are French. That is because preparing a delicious soup is a process of creating luscious layers of flavor, each layer steeped in centuries-old French cooking tradition. Special care and attention need to be taken each step of the journey. Making soup is the pinnacle of cooking, and in my opinion, there is nothing more satisfying to make. Cajoling sweetness from a pot full of thinly sliced caramelized onions for a French onion soup; braising a bœuf en daube (beef stew) until it is so tender it melts with each bite; stirring, chopping, dicing, seasoning—it's all part of making soup. It is a very tactile kind of cooking that thoroughly stimulates the senses (especially smell) and mandates frequent tasting and seasoning.

Soups and stews are also quintessentially French because they embrace and embody a tenet every good French cook knows: waste nothing! Stocks (the first step in most soups and also most sauces) are cooked from bones,

meat trimmings, fish heads, and unwanted vegetable bits such as bitter green leek leaves and tired carrots, and later strained.

Even with the cooking maxim about the easiest things being the hardest to make, there is no reason to be afraid of making soups. Indeed, making soups and stews should be pure joy, as long as you respect the method for each type of soup explored and explained in the chapters of this book. Fortunately, French chefs have honed and perfected them for us. So, now is the time to pull out your favorite sturdy soup pot and get cooking.

As with all things French, presentation is a big deal. A lot more than just sloshing soup into a bowl, it is carefully ladled into a pretty bowl or tureen (if served tableside) and often accompanied by pretty, petite garnishes in the form of herbs, croutons, etc. And all hot soup must be served very hot, fresh from a pot at a low boil. Cold soups (see chapter 3), conversely, do not have to be fresh from the fridge, but do need to be chilled.

No matter what you're cooking, always try to cook with love and joy in your heart and taste and adjust seasonings all along the way. Your food will taste better and you will enjoy the process that much more. These were lessons taught to me by a very sage and talented chef, Jean Claude Boucheret, when I was a student at Le Cordon Bleu in Paris, many moons ago. And he was right.

A Few Words on Using This Book

Because I am a staunch believer in the importance of seasoning along the way, and seasoning to personal taste, I do not tell readers how much salt and pepper to add, only when it is important to do so, which relates to building those layers of flavor. In the rare instance when I specify an amount, it is only because there is an element in the recipe where measuring the seasoning ahead is important. As far as salt and pepper go, I use only kosher or sea salt and almost always season with freshly ground black pepper, though a few recipes in this book call for ground white pepper.

Whenever possible, make your own stocks (see chapter 1). Many of the recipes in this book are built quickly from vegetable scraps from the ingredients used in the soup—again, building flavor and minimizing waste. If you need to use a commercial stock (and there are some good ones out there), buy only low sodium or no sodium versions, and try to avoid using them for any kind of consommé, where the stock is the core flavor element, sometimes reduced down and concentrated.

Finally, when cooking with wine, use only a wine you would drink and never buy cooking wine; it is full of salt and chemicals, which are definitely not friends to excellent French cooking.

Equipements pour la Préparation des Soupes et Potages

Equipment for Preparing Soups and Stews

China cap—This is a cone-shaped strainer with small holes. It is used to do the initial straining of stocks and some soups to remove any solid matter or stray bits such as bones and vegetables. Its name is derived from the shape of the hats worn by the Chinese. Available online and at specialty gourmet shops.

Chinois—Similar to a China cap, this is very important piece of equipment in a soup-and-stew kitchen. It has a longer cone shape than a China cap and an extremely fine sieve. It is used to remove the solids that made it through the first pass of the China cap. It helps ensure a flawless, silky texture in sauces, stocks, custards, and more. Available online and at specialty gourmet shops.

Ladle—A deep, broad ladle is essential for skimming stocks and soups. A ladle also helps guide the liquid through both a China cap and a chinois, through gentle swirling and pressing motions.

Whisk—A whisk is a must-have in any kitchen but comes in especially handy in soup preparation, particularly for blending the roux for cream soups and bisques. A medium-size, narrow whisk will do the trick.

Best-quality roasting pan—For achieving a nice golden color on the bones and vegetables and to create flavor and color in brown stocks, a roasting pan is helpful. I recommend a heavy-bottom, stainless steel roasting pan, ideally with a copper bottom for even heat distribution.

Stockpot—For the home kitchen, a good-quality 8- to 12-quart stock pot should do the trick. The sides are straight and tall to help regulate tempered evaporation and reduction.

Dutch oven—For a stock or a large batch of soup, I rely on my 8-quart Dutch oven, but for most of the soups and stews in this book, my 5 1/2-quart Dutch oven was just right. A Dutch oven (called a *cocotte,* in French) is an exceptionally sturdy cooking vessel, typically constructed with fairly straight sides, a cast-iron interior, and coated with ceramic. Mine are perhaps the most used items (besides knives) of everything in my kitchen. They can cook on the stovetop for soups and also do beautifully in the oven for the long, slow braises used for many of the stews in this book. Le Creuset is my brand of choice, but there are other brands available that cost less. Buy the best you can afford. You will find yourself relying on it a lot for the recipes in this book. Alternatively, a sturdy soup pot will work just fine.

Saucepans—A collection of medium and large straight-sided saucepans will facilitate refrigerator storage of soups, as well as reheating and putting finishing touches on seasoning. Look for best-quality stainless steel with a copper bottom for even heat convection.

Stacked mixing bowls—These are an added bonus in any kitchen and are handy when straining soups. Nonreactive bowls, such as glass, work best.

Food processor—Food processors, though not mandatory, are a huge aid in the soup kitchen for making quick work of purées and more.

Traditional blender/ immersion blender—For puréeing soups, I find a traditional blender works well, especially for really chunky soups. With a traditional blender, be careful to start with mostly solids for the purée, adding the broth as you go, or you risk literally blowing its top. This is why I rely so heavily on my restaurant-grade hand-held immersion blender. You stand it straight up in the soup pot, turn it on, and the purée happens in the very same pot. It does a wonderful job aerating and puréeing most soups, and because of the way it works, it means you have to clean only one pot. Of these and a food processor, if you can only afford one for your soup kitchen, go with the hand-held immersion blender.

Good-quality knives—All kitchens should be equipped with at least a paring knife and an 8-to-12-inch chef's knife. For cutting up bones and stocks, the latter will work, but a really heavy, nice-quality cleaver is even better. Keep them sharp.

Cheesecloth—It is helpful, though not necessary by any measure, to have this finely woven cloth at the ready. Lining a China cap or chinois with cheesecloth will ensure that not a single solid tidbit—such as a peppercorn or a shred of a vegetable or herb—makes its way into a silky, elegant soup such as a bisque or cream variety.

LES FONDS
Stocks

Fonds, or stocks, are the starting point for many French soups. Because stock is often the primary ingredient in soup, it is crucial that its quality be top-notch (rich in flavor and color)—especially when the stock itself is the flavor star, as is the case with consommés (page 61), French Onion Soup (page 24), Bouillabaisse (page 40), and many others. As with anything in the kitchen, if you begin and end with something subpar, chances are pretty good your soup will be too.

As you prepare your soup stock pantry, think like a French cook. One of their principal mantras is to avoid waste, *avant tout!* ("before all"). When using more expensive and harder to find produce like fennel or leeks, clean and store the parts that are rarely used in the soup itself, such as the dark green leek leaves or fennel fronds. These parts should never be discarded, but rather well cleaned and stored in your freezer for later use in a vegetable stock or to finish another stock with related flavors. The same goes for fish bones and crustacean shells (especially lobster and shrimp). Depending on where you live, these can be tricky and expensive to access at the last minute, so whenever you serve lobster or shrimp, save and freeze the well-rinsed and cleaned shells. And see Day-After-Christmas Turkey Soup (page 46) as a way to make a delicious stock from the roasted turkey carcass when the holidays come around.

Stocks derive their flavor from the most basic of ingredients—bones, vegetables, crustacean shells, meat, or a combination of some of these—simmered gently together. Stock variations included here are:

Brown Stock—made with browned beef or veal bones and classic vegetable aromatics (ingredients that add aroma and flavor, classically, onion, leek, carrots, and celery).

White Veal Stock—prepared with veal bones and classic vegetable aromatics, but the bones and vegetables are not browned. It is often used in white and cream-based sauces such as béchamel and velouté to enhance flavor.

Chicken Stock—made with skin-on chicken meat, chicken bones, and classic vegetable aromatics.

Turkey Stock—made with a chopped turkey carcass and classic vegetable aromatics.

Vegetable Stock—typically made with classic vegetable aromatics and sometimes leftover bits of other mild vegetables, such as mushrooms.

Fumet—fish stock made with fish bones, heads, tails, and classic vegetable aromatics, minus the carrots.

Techniques vary for different kinds of stock, but the theme is basically the same—produce maximum flavor and gelatin extraction (if bones are used) with minimal ingredients. It's also another very practical way to avoid waste, by putting otherwise unsexy by-products from the kitchen to good use.

The idea with stocks is to make them into subtle, flavor-layered versions of their name. For example, a beef stock should taste and smell intensely of beef, with subtle whispers of the vegetables and herbs with which it is cooked. Typically, the core vegetable aromatics of classical French cooking include onion, carrots (though not in a fish stock), leek, celery, and maybe a bit of garlic, plus a *bouquet garni* (herb bundle) of thyme, parsley, and bay leaves. The ratio of vegetables to bones and cooking liquid needs to be respected in every stock you prepare. Even though stocks are useful for using up odds and ends, if you end up throwing two pounds of tired carrots into a stock prepared with two pounds of beef marrow bones and beef scraps, your "beef" stock will end up tasting more like tired-carrot soup. Which, as one of my instructors at Le Cordon Bleu used to say, "*n'est pas bon!*"

In restaurant kitchens, long-cooked stocks (such as beef or veal) are often put on to cook at an extremely low simmer overnight and left unattended, to be strained and skimmed the following morning for use later in the day. You can try this method at home, but I like being there to oversee the entire production and, perhaps more importantly, to inhale the splendid aromas. Also, the skimming of fat and protein as it forms in a simmering stock is crucial to its flavor and visual clarity (more on this in Brown Stocks, below).

Most stocks store very well in the refrigerator for several days or in the freezer for several months, with the exception of *fumet*, which should be used the day it is made. Storing in one- or two-cup containers makes using the stocks later more convenient.

While some very good store-bought stocks are available and will do in a pinch, it is impossible to believe that the quality will be as good as what you can make at home. And the inclusion of chemicals and excess sodium can really clobber the flavor of a good soup, especially one involving a reduced stock. But the real reward in making homemade stock is the process—cathartic, sensual, slow, and so wonderfully fragrant. You can't get that in a box!

Let's take a closer look at each type of stock and how to make them the very best launching pads for many stellar soups to come.

LES FONDS BRUNS—
BŒUF ET VEAU
Brown Stocks–Beef and Veal

Beef and veal are arguably the most crucial stocks because they are so widely used, and they are prepared exactly the same way. The only difference is that the former uses beef bones and the latter uses veal bones. It is important for flavor reasons to get a little meat in there too. Because veal can be expensive to purchase and hard to find, I recommend using a combination of some of the cheapest, most flavorful, and most accessible cuts. For beef stock, I like a combination of beef

marrowbones and bone-in beef short ribs. For veal stock, I find that shanks work best. For either, if they are not already cut into 2- to 3-inch-thick disks, ask your butcher to do the job. The more exposure the pan has to the marrow and bones, the more gelatin will be released, which will add the desired viscosity to the stock. There is no reason to get fussy about perfectly shaped, petite vegetable cuts. These will cook for a very long time; so chunky is desirable, lest they cook down and into the stock, rendering it a kind of undesirable vegetable soup. Also, they will ultimately be discarded, so no one will see them.

The first step—very important—is to get the bones and vegetables a nice golden brown. This can be done on the stovetop in a stockpot, but I find the best results begin in a roasting pan on top of the stove (using two burners) and finish in a hot oven. After that, the roasting pan is deglazed with wine and finished with water before the long cooking process (5 to 8 hours) begins on the stovetop in a stockpot.

It is tempting to season a stock, but classically, stocks are not seasoned at all. Because they are often reduced (concentrating flavor), the seasoning is done at the time the stock is being prepared and finished. In my kitchen, I break slightly from tradition and suggest you do the same. A tiny pinch of salt and a dash of black pepper form a nice flavor jump-start in the early cooking process and browning of the bones and meat.

Skimming—When beef or veal stock first comes to a boil before being reduced to a simmer, the proteins and fats from the meat and bones will begin to rise to the surface in the form of froth or foam. This needs to be removed, or it will re-absorb into the stock, causing a cloudy, murky bitterness. Leave a small bowl half full of fresh water and a shallow ladle near your stockpot. When foam comes up, dip the ladle just under the surface of the foam, skim it off, and return the ladle to the water bowl. Repeat several times in the first half hour of cooking, and later, about every 30 minutes. Do be careful not to skim too deeply below the layer of the scum or you will be removing valuable stock.

After this, it is a patient waiting game, as the stock just barely simmers (avoid boiling altogether after the initial boil), emitting its gorgeous aromas along the way. This is a great

time to grab a good book and enjoy your fragrant handiwork.

Finish the stock by straining through a China cap and then a chinois (extremely fine mesh). Refrigerate shortly after preparation; it will store very well for a few days in the refrigerator or months in the freezer. Discard the vegetables or add to the compost pile. Pull the delightfully braised and tender meat from the bone and toss it in a steak sauce to prepare a simple Sloppy Joe mixture. (Marrowbones do not splinter and are canine friendly, but be careful not to share the very small ones, as a dog may choke on them.)

FOND DE BŒUF
Beef Stock
(MAKES ABOUT 8 TO 10 CUPS)

The roasting of the bones and veggies renders this versatile, fragrant stock the rich color of roasted chestnuts. Skimming, slow simmering, and straining ensure beautiful clarity and deep beef flavor that will enhance any beef or meat-friendly sauce.

2 tablespoons olive oil

2 tablespoons unsalted butter

2 pounds beef marrowbones, cut into 2-inch-thick rounds

1 1/2 pounds bone-in beef short ribs, coarsely chopped

Tiny pinch of sea salt or kosher salt

Pinch of freshly ground black pepper

1 large onion, quartered

2 large ribs celery, cut into 2-inch lengths

1 large leek, white part only, cleaned and cut into 2-inch lengths

2 carrots, peeled and cut into 2-inch lengths

2 tablespoons tomato paste

1 cup full-bodied red wine (e.g., a Merlot or Cabernet Sauvignon)

14 cups cold water (or just enough to barely cover the bones and vegetables)

3 cloves garlic

1 bouquet garni (several sprigs fresh thyme, fresh parsley, and 2 bay leaves)

5 peppercorns

Preheat oven to 500 degrees F.

In a large, sturdy, nonstick roasting pan, heat olive oil and butter over medium-high heat (using two burners if necessary) until bubbling vigorously. Add the marrowbones and short ribs. Season with salt and ground pepper. Brown, turning every few minutes to color all sides, cooking for a total of about 10 minutes. Add the onion, celery, leek, and carrots, and toss to coat. Place the roasting pan on the middle rack of the preheated oven. Roast for 10 to 15 minutes, tossing once or twice to turn the vegetables. Add the tomato paste, stirring well to coat the bones and vegetables evenly. Let cook 5 to 10 minutes more. (*Note*: This is an important step to cook out the acidity of the paste).

Remove roasting pan from the oven. Return to the stovetop, with the burner(s) set on high. Deglaze the roasting pan with the red wine, stirring with a flat-edged wooden spoon to scrape up any brown bits. Cook until the wine has reduced by half.

continued >

Carefully turn out the contents of the roasting pan into an 8- to 12-quart stockpot. Add the water, garlic, bouquet garni, and peppercorns.

Bring to a boil, then reduce to a barely discernible simmer. Skim initial froth and foam carefully with a ladle and discard. Repeat 2 or 3 times during the first 30 minutes of cooking, then every 30 minutes. Cook for 5 to 8 hours, or until the stock has developed a rich flavor and color and reduced by about one-third. Carefully strain the stock through a China cap over another large pot or bowl, setting the solids aside. Strain a second time, through a chinois. Store in airtight containers in the refrigerator for up to 3 to 4 days or in the freezer for several months.

FOND BRUN DE VEAU
Brown Veal Stock

(MAKES ABOUT 8 TO 10 CUPS)

Use the same recipe as for the beef stock, but substitute 3 pounds veal shanks for the beef marrowbones and short ribs.

FUMET DE POISSON
Fish Stock
(MAKES ABOUT 6 CUPS)

Fish stock cooks relatively quickly, coming together in just 20 minutes. Make it the day you're going to use it, as it loses freshness fast. Look for bones and heads from white fish such as haddock and cod. Salmon and tuna are not good picks, since they can make the stock bitter. Don't use carrots in fish stock, as they can muddle the color.

2½ pounds fish heads and bones
1¼ cup best-quality dry white wine (e.g.,
    Chardonnay or Pinot Grigio)
1 onion, thinly sliced
1 leek, cleaned and thinly sliced

1 bouquet garni (several sprigs fresh thyme, fresh
    parsley, and 2 bay leaves)
Tiny pinch of sea salt or kosher salt
6 cups water

Combine all of the ingredients in an 8-quart Dutch oven, stockpot, or large deep skillet. Bring to a boil and reduce to a simmer, skimming initial and subsequent foam from the top, cooking for 20 minutes. Strain through a China cap first, then through a chinois. Reserve warm or in the refrigerator until ready to use.

FOND DE VOLAILLE
Chicken or Turkey Stock

(MAKES ABOUT 8 TO 10 CUPS)

Though better-quality commercial chicken and, to a lesser extent, turkey stocks are more ubiquitous than veal and beef, making your own is going to ensure the quality and produce the olfactory and gustatory pleasure of preparing it. I recommend starting with a whole 3- to 4-pound chicken (or the carcass of an 8-pound-plus turkey). Rinse it, pat it dry, and cut it into smaller pieces with a sharp cleaver or chef's knife. The easiest way to approach the job is to cut the breasts away from the spine and ribs, then cut each breast in two. Separate the legs from the carcass and cut those in two as well. Finally, hack at the ribs and spine to break them up into a few pieces. The goal is to expose cut bone to maximize flavor and gelatin content in the stock. If you don't feel comfortable doing this, ask the butcher to, or buy pre-cut meat with the skin on.

After straining the solids from the stock, save the meat off the bones for salad or soup (Note: There will be considerably more meat from the chicken than the turkey). The stock should be fragrant and a clear, pale yellow color. Unlike the veal and beef stock recipes, chicken bones and vegetables are only very lightly browned.

2 tablespoons olive oil

2 tablespoons unsalted butter

1 (3- to 4-pound) whole chicken, cut up into 8 pieces (or chopped turkey carcass for a turkey stock)

Tiny pinch of sea salt or kosher salt

Freshly ground black pepper

1 large onion, quartered

2 carrots, peeled and cut into 2-inch lengths

2 large ribs celery, cut into 2-inch lengths

1 large leek, white and green parts, cleaned and cut into 2-inch lengths

3 cloves garlic

1 bouquet garni (several sprigs fresh thyme, fresh parsley, and 2 bay leaves)

1/2 cup good-quality white wine (e.g., Pinot Grigio or Chardonnay)

14-16 cups cold water (just enough to barely cover the chicken or turkey and vegetables)

5 peppercorns

Heat together the olive oil and butter in an 8- to 10-quart stockpot on the stovetop over medium-high heat. When bubbling, add the cut-up chicken (or turkey for a turkey stock). Season very lightly with salt and pepper. Sauté lightly, stirring once or twice, for about 5 minutes. Add the onion, carrots, celery, and leek, stirring to coat. Sauté lightly for an additional 2 minutes. Add the garlic, bouquet garni, and white wine. Increase heat to high and reduce the wine by half. Add the water and peppercorns.

Bring to a boil, then reduce heat to a barely discernible simmer. Skim the initial layer of foam with a ladle and discard. Repeat 2 or 3 times during the first 30 minutes of cooking, then every 30 minutes. Cook uncovered for 3 to 4 hours, or until liquid is reduced by about one-third.

Carefully strain the stock through a China cap over another large pot or bowl, setting the solids aside. Repeat a second time through a chinois. Store in airtight containers in the refrigerator up to 3 to 4 days or in the freezer for several months.

FOND BLANC DE VEAU
White Veal Stock
(MAKES ABOUT 8 TO 10 CUPS)

Used in some soups and stews, the goal here is to extract the flavor of the veal and vegetables without "coloring" the stock through browning, roasting, etc. Prepare it the same way as the chicken stock, except substitute 2 pounds veal shank or marrowbones for the whole chicken.

CHAPTER 2

LES SOUPES CLASSIQUES
ET VARIATIONS
Classic Soups and Variations

As with fashion, language, architecture, and all types of art creating strong, soul-stirring human impressions, some French soups become classics for a reason. It is because they are unforgettably delicious interpretations of French taste, culture, ingredients, and regions. In this chapter, we prepare some of the most well-known soups, including French Onion and Bouillabaisse (who could say *non* to either?). We'll also call on some lesser known but equally *délicieuse* soups, like the verdant Provençal Vegetable Soup with Basil Pesto and earthy French Green Lentil Soup with Bacon. Also in this chapter are a few interpretations of other classic French dishes not usually served as soups, including my personal favorite, an apple-spiked fondue, Three-Cheese and Cider Soup with Apples and Four-Spice Croutons.

Soupe au Pistou
Provençal Vegetable Soup with Basil Pesto
(MAKES 8 TO 10 SERVINGS)

Provence reveres garlic, and this soup pays homage to its humble, fragrant cloves. The garlic is blended with fresh basil leaves, Parmesan, and pine nuts to form a sauce (or pistou) that swirls its way into every bite of this veggie-packed soup. The pistou can be made ahead, but it's important to prevent exposure to air, as that will render it an ugly gray color. Top the container with a layer of olive oil and seal with plastic wrap. Pistou also freezes beautifully.

You can make the soup base ahead. However, cook the pasta in the soup just before serving, and swirl in the pesto at the very end; otherwise, the pasta will become soggy and the pesto color could turn. This is an especially delicious soup during summer when all of its ingredients are at their seasonal peak. Take time to chop them all neatly at about the same size for a prettier look and more even cooking.

For the pistou:

2 cups fresh basil leaves, packed

1 cup fresh parsley leaves, packed

4 cloves garlic

1 cup grated Parmigiano-Reggiano cheese

1/2 cup pine nuts

Salt and freshly ground black pepper

1 cup best-quality extra virgin olive oil

For the soup:

3 tablespoons extra virgin olive oil

1/2 cup finely chopped red onion

2 medium ribs celery, finely chopped

2 medium carrots, peeled and finely diced (see
   Brunoise, page 52)

1 fennel bulb, stalks and fronds removed (and
   reserved for garnish), cored and finely diced

Salt and freshly ground black pepper

1/2 cup good-quality white wine (e.g., Chardonnay)

3 small zucchini, ends trimmed, finely diced (see
   Brunoise, page 52)

3 small tomatoes, finely chopped

4 cups vegetable stock

4 cups water

1 (15.5-ounce) can cannellini beans with juices

Pinch of red pepper flakes

6 sprigs fresh thyme, bundled with kitchen string

1 cup dried elbow pasta

For the pistou, combine all ingredients except the olive oil in the bowl of a food processor fitted with a metal blade or a blender, and pulse 20 times. With the motor running, stream the olive oil slowly through the mouth of the processor or blender until well combined. Taste, and adjust seasonings as needed. Store as suggested in the recipe headnote.

For the soup, heat the olive oil over medium-high heat in a 5 1/2-quart Dutch oven or similarly sized pot. Add the onion, celery, carrots, fennel, and a generous pinch of salt and pepper. Stir to coat. Reduce the heat to medium. Cook uncovered for 10 minutes, or until the vegetables have started to soften, stirring once or twice. Add the wine, increase the heat to high, and reduce the wine by half. Add the zucchini, tomatoes, and another dash of salt and pepper. Cook another 5 minutes. Add the vegetable stock and water. Bring to a boil over high heat, then reduce to medium heat and simmer. Add half of the cannellini beans with their juices. Smash the remaining half in the can with the back of a fork to coarsely purée. Add this to the soup along with the red pepper flakes, thyme sprig bundle, and a generous dash of salt and pepper. Cook for 10 minutes. (*Note*: If preparing in advance, stop here and cool the soup; store overnight in the refrigerator, covered.) Add the elbow pasta to the soup and cook until al dente, about 10 minutes.

To serve, remove the thyme sprig bundle and discard. Serve the soup in shallow bowls. Swirl about 1 tablespoon of pistou into each bowl just before serving, or pass pistou at the table. If desired, garnish with a fennel frond.

FENNEL CORING TIPS

To prep and core fennel, cut the hard, spindly stalks away from the bulb. Save the pretty fronds for decoration. To remove the tough core, place the fennel bulb straight up, sitting on its bottom. Cut it in half vertically. You'll see the whitish, triangular core in the center. It will be tough. Cut down on both sides with a chef's knife and remove it. Proceed to chop as directed.

SOUPE À L'OIGNON
French Onion Soup

(MAKES 6 SERVINGS)

Hardly anything I can think of trumps the utterly simple deliciousness of a well-prepared French onion soup. Like all dishes with very few ingredients, the key is making each one count. For an exquisite French onion soup, it boils down to three things: a top-quality, rich and dark beef stock; slowly caramelized onions; and Gruyère or Comté cheese for topping. Therefore, if at all possible, make your own stock; don't rush the onions; and go for the best-quality imported cheese you can afford. Processed Swiss will work in a pinch, but the flavor and color will be diluted. The heady layers of sweet onions marrying with nutty, bubbling cheese and the rich broth make this an ideal soup for entertaining. All of the components can be made ahead and put together at the last minute before serving, and I've never met a soul (French or otherwise) that doesn't wholly appreciate a stunning French onion soup.

Special equipment: Six 1¹/₃-cup ovenproof bowls or ramekins

2 tablespoons extra virgin olive oil

2 tablespoons unsalted butter

3 large sweet onions (preferably Vidalia) or regular white onions, halved and thinly sliced (about 6 cups)

3 cloves garlic, smashed and finely chopped

Salt and freshly ground black pepper

2 tablespoons chopped fresh thyme leaves

³/₄ cup good-quality white wine (e.g., Chardonnay)

¹/₂ cup dry vermouth

1 tablespoon all-purpose flour

4 cups best-quality unsalted beef stock (preferably homemade, see Beef Stock, page 15)

For the croutons and garnish:

12 slices day-old French baguette bread, cut into ¹/₂-inch-thick slices

2 tablespoons olive oil

3 cups grated Gruyère or Comté cheese

Thyme sprigs for garnish, optional

In a 5¹/₂-quart Dutch oven or similarly sized soup pot, melt the olive oil and butter together over medium-high heat. Add the onions, garlic, and a generous dash of salt and pepper. Stir to coat. Reduce heat to medium-low and cook, stirring occasionally, until all of the onion liquid is cooked off and the onions have become quite soft, about 25 minutes. Add the thyme and continue cooking until the onions turn golden and caramelize, about 10 minutes. The onions should be a pale, golden color, not deeply browned, which would render them bitter. Taste, and adjust salt and pepper as needed.

continued >

Increase heat to high and add the wine, stirring to pick up any brown bits; reduce by half. Add the vermouth and reduce by half again. Sprinkle the flour evenly over the soup, stirring to mix in, and cook for 1 minute. Add the beef stock and stir. Bring to a boil and then reduce to a simmer, cooking another 15 minutes, uncovered.

Meanwhile, turn the broiler on high. Arrange the bread in a single layer on a baking sheet. Drizzle each side lightly with olive oil and rub it into the bread. Place the sheet on the top shelf and broil until the bread is just golden on each side, turning once.

You can stop here and store the soup separately from the garnishes overnight in the refrigerator, or continue to the finish. To serve, taste the soup again and adjust seasonings if necessary. Ladle boiling-hot soup into each bowl or ramekin. Top each with 2 or 3 croutons and about $1/2$ cup grated cheese. Arrange on a baking sheet and broil on the middle rack until the cheese is golden and bubbly, about 4 to 6 minutes. Serve immediately, garnishing with fresh thyme sprigs if desired.

Soupe aux Trois Fromages et au Cidre avec Pommes et Croûtons de Quatre Épices

Three-Cheese and Cider Soup with Apples and Four-Spice Croutons

(MAKES 4 TO 6 SERVINGS)

One chilly winter afternoon many years ago in Chalabre, France, I spent a few hours with my friend Olivier as his apprentice, studying the nuances of preparing fondue. Fondue, derived from the French fondre *(to melt), can be made with cheese, chocolate, or just about anything that melts. Olivier was focusing on the cheese version. For him, the most important part was the cheese selection (he loves Comté) and the ratio of cheese to wine. His silky, fragrant concoction was one of the best things I have ever eaten. It was the inspiration for this soup. Like Olivier's, it uses Comté, but also nutty Gruyère and Parmesan cheeses, for sturdy aged flavor. Instead of wine, a splash of fresh apple cider gives a sweet, acidic edge that is recalled with fresh, thinly sliced apples used as the dipping conduit to eat the soup, which is topped with crunchy croutons seasoned with piquant quatre épices (see page 29). The soup base and croutons can be made ahead and stored a day or two in the refrigerator and in a sealed container, respectively. Prep the apples at the last minute before serving.*

3 tablespoons unsalted butter

1 large shallot, finely chopped

3 cloves garlic, finely chopped

Salt and freshly ground black pepper

3 tablespoons all-purpose flour

4 cups unsalted Chicken Stock (see page 18) or vegetable stock

3/4 cup fresh apple cider (not concentrate)

1 cup grated Comté cheese

1/2 cup grated Gruyère cheese

1/4 cup grated Parmesan cheese

2/3 cup heavy cream

For the croutons:

2 tablespoons olive oil

1/2 small day-old baguette, cut into 1/4-inch cubes

1 1/2 teaspoons quatre épices (see sidebar and recipe, page 29)

Generous pinch of salt

For the garnish:

2 Granny Smith apples

Juice of 1/2 lemon

In a 5 1/2-quart Dutch oven or similarly sized pot, melt the butter over medium heat. Add the shallot, garlic, and a generous dash of salt and pepper. Stir to combine. Cook until the vegetables are just softened, 5 minutes. Add the flour, stir to coat vegetables, and cook for 1 minute. Whisk in the

continued >

stock and bring to a boil over high heat. Add the apple cider and reduce by approximately ¼ cup. Reduce heat to medium. Stir in the three cheeses until melted. Simmer another 5 minutes. Add the cream and cook gently over medium heat for 10 minutes, whisking occasionally. Taste, and adjust seasonings as needed.

Meanwhile, prepare the croutons. In a large sauté pan, heat the olive oil over medium-high heat until it just begins to bubble and move across the bottom of the pan. Add the bread cubes and toss to coat completely with the oil. Sprinkle the quatre épices evenly over the croutons. Toss to coat. Season lightly with salt. Continue cooking until the croutons are light golden brown. Remove from the pan and drain on paper towels. Reserve warm. (*Note*: Once the croutons have cooled, you can seal them in a plastic container and hold a few days at room temperature. Reheat briefly in a 425-degree oven or in a sauté pan over medium heat to crisp before serving.)

Just before serving, slice the apples and toss with the lemon juice. To serve, ladle the hot soup into shallow bowls. Top each with a small mound of warm croutons. Arrange 3 or 4 slices of apple on the edge of each bowl, or arrange on a plate, for dipping into the soup.

QUATRE ÉPICES WITH SPICE BLEND RECIPE

Quatre épices, or "four spices" is a spice blend that pops up frequently in French cooking, particularly in savory dishes, such as soups, stews, charcuterie, and pâtés, but also sometimes in bread and pastries. It is difficult to find in the States but easy enough to make using a blend of spices commonly found in home pantries. I suggest making it in small batches and keeping a jar in your spice drawer for easy access. Here is the recipe:

1 tablespoon ground white pepper   1 tablespoon ground nutmeg

1 tablespoon ground cloves   1 tablespoon ground ginger

SOUPES AUX LENTILLES DU PUY AVEC LARDONS

Puy Green Lentil Soup with Bacon

(MAKES 8 SERVINGS)

Deep in the rich volcanic soil of Auvergne, in south-central France, reside the nutrients that help create the rich flavor and color of the Puy lentils. They are extra firm and dark green, with sage-hued threads and a peppery flavor. Unlike other lentils, they hold their shape and have a firm, toothsome texture even when cooked, rather than breaking down into mushy legume puddles. Referred to as French green lentils in the United States, they are increasingly easy to find here at regular grocery stores and markets.

Be sure to rinse the lentils and pick them over for any small stones. It's okay to salt them very lightly in the beginning of the cooking process, but save the bulk of the salt for after they are cooked, as salt can harden them. A dash of cloves and dried sage give it an extra earthy, hard-to-resist flavor that works magic with the peppery quality.

8 slices bacon, cut into a $^1/_2$-inch dice (about $1^1/_2$ cups), divided

Freshly ground black pepper

1 medium onion, finely chopped

2 leeks, trimmed to 1 inch above the white part of the stalk (see The Nitty-Gritty on Leeks, page 45), halved vertically, well rinsed, and finely chopped

2 medium ribs celery, finely chopped

1 large carrot, peeled and finely chopped

3 cloves garlic, smashed and coarsely chopped

Salt

$^1/_2$ cup good-quality full-bodied red wine (e.g., Cabernet Sauvignon)

$1^1/_2$ cups French green lentils

4 cups vegetable stock

1 cup water

2 bay leaves

Generous pinch of ground cloves

$1^1/_2$ teaspoons ground sage

For the garnish:

Half of reserved cooked bacon

$^1/_4$ cup Crème Fraîche (see page 54) or sour cream

3 tablespoons finely chopped fresh parsley

Heat a $5^1/_2$-quart Dutch oven or similarly sized pot over medium-high heat. Add the diced bacon and black pepper. Cook to render fat and brown the bacon, stirring every minute or so. Reduce heat to medium-low and continue cooking the bacon until it is cooked through and nicely browned. Remove the bacon with a slotted spoon and drain on paper towels. Set aside.

continued >

Drain off all but 3 tablespoons of the bacon fat from the cooking pot. Add the onion, leek, celery, carrot, and garlic. Season very lightly with salt and pepper. Stir to coat. Cook until just softened, about 5 minutes. Deglaze with the red wine, stirring to pick up any brown bits from the bacon. Increase heat to high and reduce the wine by about half. Add the lentils, vegetable stock, water, bay leaves, ground cloves, and ground sage. Season lightly with salt and pepper. Bring to a boil over high heat and reduce to a simmer over medium-low heat. Cook uncovered until the lentils have softened to a gentle chew state (al dente), 35–40 minutes. Remove the bay leaves. Purée with an immersion or stand blender until aerated and chunky smooth.

Return purée to the pot and bring to a low simmer. If soup seems too thick, add enough water to adjust to your liking; about 1/2 to 1 cup of water should do it. Stir in half of the reserved bacon. Taste, and adjust the salt and pepper as needed.

To serve, ladle the soup into individual bowls, then garnish each with a dollop of sour cream or crème fraîche and a sprinkle of bacon and fresh parsley.

Note: The soup can be made ahead and refrigerated for 1 or 2 days or frozen for up to 2 months.

HOW TO PREP GARLIC

At Le Cordon Bleu, my chefs were insistent about removing the tough green stem in the center of all but the youngest garlic cloves. They were adamant that its bitter flavor would spoil the soup, or the sauce, or whatever we were making. Despite this training, I feel that it's fine to leave it in when using garlic in very small quantities, say one or two cloves. However, when using large quantities (as in the following recipe), I would definitely take it out.

The process is simple. Smash the garlic with the thickest part of your chef's knife blade, pressing down with the weight of your arm. It will naturally break into two or three pieces. Remove the green core and discard. This will also break the skin off the garlic clove, so you can carefully peel and remove it. To chop, gather the garlic into a pile and chop repeatedly, guiding the blade of your knife so that all pieces are very fine and about the same size.

AÏGO BOUIDO
Garlic Soup

(MAKES 6 SERVINGS)

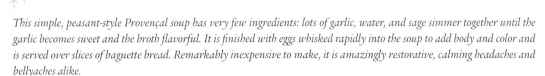

This simple, peasant-style Provençal soup has very few ingredients: lots of garlic, water, and sage simmer together until the garlic becomes sweet and the broth flavorful. It is finished with eggs whisked rapidly into the soup to add body and color and is served over slices of baguette bread. Remarkably inexpensive to make, it is amazingly restorative, calming headaches and bellyaches alike.

Garlic lovers will go "fou" for this soup! I change up the traditional formula just a bit, adding vegetable stock and saffron for flavor and substituting rosemary for sage, but feel free to use sage if you like. To keep the fat content low, I used egg whites instead of whole eggs. A splash of vinegar at the end gives a tiny acidic punch.

2 tablespoons unsalted butter

2 tablespoons olive oil

1 medium onion, quartered and thinly sliced

2 heads garlic, or about 30 cloves, green core removed (see How to Prep Garlic, page 32), thinly sliced on a diagonal

Salt and freshly ground black pepper

4 cups vegetable stock

2 cups water

10 saffron threads

1 tablespoon finely chopped fresh rosemary leaves

4 egg whites

$^1/_2$ teaspoon red wine vinegar

For the garnish:

12 ($^1/_2$-inch-thick) diagonal slices baguette bread

$^1/_2$ cup grated Parmesan or Gruyère cheese

In a 5$^1/_2$-quart Dutch oven or similarly sized pot, melt the butter and olive oil over medium-high heat. Add onion, garlic, and a sprinkling of salt and freshly ground black pepper. Stir to coat. Reduce heat to medium-low and continue cooking the mixture until softened, about 15 minutes. Do not let the onions or garlic turn color. They should taste sweet and be very soft when done. Add the vegetable stock, water, saffron, rosemary, and another layer of salt and pepper. Bring to a boil over high heat, and then reduce heat to medium-low and simmer uncovered another 20 minutes.

Whisk the egg whites together in a small bowl. Stream the egg whites into the simmering soup, whisking rapidly until thin strands of eggs have formed throughout the soup. Add vinegar. Taste, and adjust seasonings as needed.

To serve, place 1 or 2 baguette slices in each bowl. Top with very hot soup. Sprinkle the top with a tablespoon or so of the grated cheese.

Note: The soup stores very well refrigerated in a sealed container for up to 2 days.

SOUPE RUSTIQUE AUX LÉGUMES D'HIVER
Rustic Winter Vegetable Soup

(MAKES 8 TO 10 SERVINGS)

Far from barren, the French winter vegetable garden (at least in most parts of France) is verdant with savory root vegetables, cabbage, sturdy greens, and more. Or they are holding safely in storage until spring. This simple and tremendously satisfying soup is typique *of the kind of soup you might find simmering on stoves in cooler months, particularly in the French country-side villages such as Chalabre, in Languedoc-Roussillon, where I lived for many blessed years.*

This soup is utterly French in its frugality, complete lack of waste, and rustic presentation. Because so much of the flavor is derived from the vegetables during a long, slow simmer, it is prepared with fresh tap or spring water, as opposed to stock or broth. You will note in the recipe that I provide a measured amount of salt and pepper, in a departure from my usual "taste and adjust as you go" plan. That's because the vegetables need a fairly large amount of seasoning to pull out their sweetness and layered flavors. Finished with a flutter of chopped fresh parsley, lemon zest, and a splash of the most fruity, fragrant olive oil you can find, this rustic soup is fit for a king. It can be puréed if you like, but I prefer it on the chunky side. Either way, aim to keep the vegetables all about the same size for even cooking time and presentation.

1 medium celery root* (see Celeriac, page 36), peeled and cut into 1-inch chunks

1 fennel bulb (fronds and stems removed), halved, cored (see Fennel Coring Tips, page 23), and cut into 1-inch chunks

2 leeks, trimmed to just 1 inch above the white part (see The Nitty-Gritty on Leeks, page 45), halved vertically, well rinsed, and cut into 1-inch lengths

1 large Yukon gold potato, scrubbed and cut into 1-inch chunks

3 large carrots, peeled and cut into 1-inch lengths (Cut the wider ends in half to approximate the size of the more slender part of the carrot)

2 medium ribs celery, cut into 1-inch lengths

1 medium onion, halved and cut into 1-inch chunks

3 medium cloves garlic, smashed and minced

8 cups water

2 bay leaves

1 teaspoon fennel seeds

1 tablespoon salt

1 teaspoon freshly ground black pepper, plus more to taste

1 tablespoon fruity extra virgin olive oil

Fat bundle of parsley stems, tied with kitchen string

1/4 cup finely chopped fresh parsley

Zest of 1 lemon

For the garnish:

More fruity extra virgin oil, about 1/4 cup

1/4 cup grated Parmesan cheese

continued >

In a 5½-quart Dutch oven or similarly sized pot, add the celery root, fennel, leeks, potato, carrots, celery, onion, garlic, water, bay leaves, fennel seeds, salt, pepper, olive oil, and parsley stem bundle. Stir to combine. Bring to a boil on high heat. Reduce to medium-low and cook uncovered at a low simmer for 2 hours, or until the vegetables are very tender. Taste, and adjust seasonings as needed. Remove and discard the bay leaves and parsley bundle.

Note: You can stop the soup at this point, cool, and refrigerate covered for 1 to 2 days.

Just before serving, bring the soup to a low boil and reheat thoroughly. Finish with the chopped parsley and lemon zest. Serve in individual bowls or in a tureen, garnished with a generous drizzle of fruity olive oil and the Parmesan cheese.

If you have trouble finding celery root, substitute rutabaga. Its sweetness would be well suited to this wonderful soup.

Variations: Cabbage, rutabaga, parsnips, turnips, and fresh pumpkin or another hearty winter squash would make nice additions to this soup.

CELERIAC

Celeriac is the French word for celery root, which is exactly what this subtly flavored vegetable is: the root of the celery plant. When cooked, it has a flavor that is vaguely reminiscent of fresh celery and has the fluffy texture of a potato. It's a cool-weather root vegetable, fresh in fall and winter, and stores relatively well refrigerated. At the grocery store or market, look for firm, round roots, heavy and dense for their size. It has a dappled, dimpled, ugly outer skin that is usually partially dusted with dirt.

Like rutabaga, celeriac has two skins: an outer skin, and a thicker second skin about ⅛ inch thick. To peel celery root, trim both ends and discard. Place one of the flat, trimmed ends on your cutting board, and cut through both skins with a small chef's knife, turning the root as you go until the entire root is peeled. Rinse the root well and clean off your cutting surface. Proceed to chop and cook as needed.

SOUPE À LA BRANDADE DE MORUE AVEC DES LARDONS
Salt Cod, Potato, and Garlic Soup with Bacon
(SERVES 6 TO 8)

Salt cod has been the mainstay of Mediterranean diets for centuries. Once plentiful in the Atlantic embracing the shores of France, Spain, and Italy, it was an inexpensive fish that preserved well packed in salt and shelved in a cool corner for several winter months. Consequently, it is the cornerstone of many classic dishes, including Brandade de Morue in France—a heady blend of mashed potatoes with lots of garlic and olive oil, puréed with salt cod, and baked into a soufflé-like puff. It is one of my all-time favorite French comfort foods, and I frequently inhaled the stuff at a bistro around the corner from my first Paris apartment. Though not a classic soup, per se, this recipe is an interpretation of the classic French Brandade in soup form.

Finding the cod may be your biggest challenge. Look for it in the refrigerator/freezer section of your market, or Hispanic or Italian groceries, or visit www.tienda.com. Plan ahead for the desalting process, which takes a day or two.

The texture of salt cod (versus fresh cod) is meaty. It pairs beautifully with the potatoes, thyme, cream, and bacon in this luscious soup. Be careful with salt as you move along with this dish. Between the cod and the bacon, it can become too salty if you're not judicious. But, then, as they say in France, if your food is too salty, it probably means you're in love. Not such a bad thing!

1 pound skinless, boneless salt cod filets (I like Bos'n brand)

1 tablespoon olive oil

6 slices bacon, cut into 1/2-inch dice

Salt and freshly ground black pepper

1 medium onion, finely chopped

2 ribs celery, finely chopped

3 large cloves garlic, smashed and finely chopped

1 teaspoon chopped fresh thyme leaves

1/2 cup good-quality white wine (e.g., Chardonnay)

2 medium Yukon gold potatoes, peeled and cut into

1-inch cubes (about 2 1/2 cups)

4 cups Fish Stock (see page 17) or best-quality boxed fish stock

2 bay leaves

1 tablespoon extra dry vermouth

1/2 cup heavy cream

For the garnish:

Reserved cooked bacon

12 sprigs fresh thyme

Two days before making the soup, begin the desalting process of the cod. Rinse well under running water. Place in a container large enough to submerge the cod filets. Cover and refrigerate. Change the water, rinsing well, at least 4 times daily for 2 days before preparing the soup. After

continued >

this process, drain the fish well. Run your index finger along the line of the filet, and pluck out any random bones and discard. Cut cod into 1-inch squares.

Heat a 5½-quart Dutch oven or similarly sized pot over medium-high heat. Add the olive oil. When bubbling, add the diced bacon. Season lightly with salt and pepper. Cook 5 to 8 minutes, or until lightly browned and all of the fat has been rendered. Remove the bacon with a slotted spoon and set aside to drain on paper towels.

Discard all but 3 tablespoons of the bacon fat from the pot. Add the onion, celery, and garlic, and a light sprinkling of salt and pepper. Cook over medium heat, stirring, until just softened, about 5 minutes. Add thyme, desalted, prepped cod, and white wine. Increase heat to high, stir well to pick up any brown bits, and reduce liquid by half.

Add the potatoes, fish stock, and bay leaves. Bring to a boil over high heat, then reduce to medium-low and continue cooking uncovered at a simmer until the potatoes are soft enough to pierce with the tip of a paring knife, about 20 to 25 minutes. Be sure to skim off and discard any foam or scum during the cooking process. Remove and discard the bay leaves.

Purée the soup with an immersion or stand blender until smooth. Reheat the soup. Taste, and adjust seasonings as needed. Add the vermouth and heavy cream. Simmer for 5 minutes.

(*Note:* The soup can be fully prepped ahead, covered, and refrigerated for 1 to 2 days before serving.) Serve in shallow bowls and garnish each with a small mound of the reserved bacon and a sprig of thyme.

BOUILLABAISSE
Provençal Fish Soup

(MAKES 8 SERVINGS)

Bouillabaisse is one of the most loved and exceptional of the classic French soups. Creating a wholly authentic bouillabaisse in the United States presents some challenges. Specifically, the lack of availability of the principal bony fish (red rascasse, grondin, conger, and dorade) of the Mediterranean Sea, especially found near Marseille, that are used to fortify and help create the fumet base. But it is possible to find some of the fish (such as lotte, or monk fish in English) that are layered into the stew and poached in the fumet. Or substitute another firm white fish such as cod, sea bass, or snapper. The fragrant soup base is always rife with the tempting aromas of saffron, fennel, fresh orange, Pernod, and tomatoes. And it is always topped with croutons and a generous dollop of wonderful garlicky rouille.

In this recipe, I fortify a really good fish fumet base (see page 17) with readily available shrimp and lobster shells, garlic, fennel, onion, tomato, thyme, and more, simmer it for a while, and strain through a chinois, pushing firmly with a ladle to help extract all flavors from the solids. These are then discarded, and the broth is finished with similar vegetables and layers of fresh fish poaching in the broth. Remember that the exact type of fish you use doesn't matter. Buy the best, freshest fish you can find and stay away from oily fish such as tuna and salmon. Scallops and shrimp are fine too. The result is dramatic and stunning—both in flavor and presentation.

Traditionally, bouillabaisse is made to serve a large crowd and is served in two separate tureens: one containing the broth topped with the croutons and rouille, and another for the fish and vegetables. I usually serve it in individual bowls (fish and vegetables together), with rouille and croutons on the side. I make the fortified fumet, croutons, and rouille a day ahead, and finish the Bouillabaisse on the day of serving.

For the fortified fumet base:

1 (1-pound) cooked lobster

3 tablespoons olive oil

1 medium onion, halved and thinly sliced

1 fennel bulb (stalks and fronds removed and reserved), thinly sliced

3 cloves garlic, smashed

Salt and freshly ground black pepper

2 teaspoons tomato paste

Shells from 1/2 pound medium-size (16-20 count) shrimp (reserve the shrimp for later use)

1/2 cup good-quality Chardonnay or another full-bodied white wine

1/4 cup Pernod (see Pernod and Pastis, page 43)

6 cups homemade Fish Stock (see page 17) or best-quality commercial fish stock

2 cups water

2 bay leaves

6 sprigs fresh thyme

Small handful of fresh parsley leaves

Stalks from fennel bulb cut into 2-inch lengths

1/4 teaspoon dried orange peel

8 saffron threads

For the croutons:

16-20 slices day-old French baguette bread, cut into 1/2-inch-thick slices

2 tablespoons olive oil

Salt and freshly ground black pepper

To finish the soup:

3 tablespoons olive oil

1 medium onion, halved and thinly sliced

1 fennel bulb, cored, quartered, and thinly sliced

1 red bell pepper, halved, seeded, and thinly sliced

3 cloves garlic, smashed and finely diced

Salt and freshly ground black pepper

$1/4$ cup freshly squeezed orange juice

3 tablespoons Pernod

Reserved fortified fumet base

1 large Yukon Gold potato, scrubbed and cut into 1-inch cubes

Generous pinch of red pepper flakes

$1/2$ pound monkfish, carefully boned and cut into 1-inch cubes

$3/4$ pound cod, carefully boned and cut into 1-inch cubes

$1/2$ pound swordfish, cut into 1-inch cubes

$1/4$ cup finely chopped fresh parsley

16 cherrystone clams, finely rinsed

For the fumet base, remove lobster tail, claws, and legs; discard the body. Smash the claws and tail with a mallet to expose meat and broken shells.

In a $5^{1}/2$-quart Dutch oven or similarly sized pot, heat the olive oil over medium-high heat. Add the onion, fennel, and garlic, and season lightly with salt and pepper. Stir to coat, and cook for 3 minutes. Add the tomato paste. Reduce heat to medium and cook through another 2 minutes. Add the lobster and shrimp shells. Stir to coat, and cook for another 2 minutes.

Increase heat to medium-high. Add the Chardonnay and reduce down to a glaze. Add the Pernod and repeat. Add the fish stock, water, bay leaves, thyme, parsley, fennel stalks, dried orange peel, and safron. Bring to a boil over high heat, and then reduce to a simmer. Cook uncovered for 30 minutes, skimming off any foam as it comes to the surface. (*Note*: It's easiest to do this with a bowl of water and a ladle. Skim off the foam with the wet ladle and pour into the bowl as you go. Discard when you're through.) Strain the liquid through a chinois into another pot, pressing firmly against the solids to extract maximum flavor. Reserve. (*Note*: It's best to make this 1 or 2 days ahead and store in the refrigerator until finishing the Bouillabaisse.)

For the croutons: Heat the broiler on high. Arrange the bread slices on a baking sheet in a single layer. Drizzle each side lightly with olive oil and rub it into the bread. Season lightly with salt and pepper on both sides. Place the sheet on the top shelf and broil until croutons are just golden; then turn and broil on the other side. Cool croutons and store in a sealed container for up to 2 days, until ready to use.

To finish the soup: In a $5^{1}/2$-quart Dutch oven or similarly sized pot, heat the olive oil over medium heat. Add the onion, fennel bulb, bell pepper, and garlic, and season lightly with salt and pepper. Stir to coat. Cook for 5 minutes, or until just softened. Add the orange juice and reduce to a glaze over medium-high heat. Repeat with the Pernod. Add the reserved, strained fumet base. Bring to a boil over high and reduce to a simmer. Add the potato and red pepper flakes, and season lightly again with salt and pepper. Simmer for 20 minutes, or until the potatoes are soft and yield easily to the tip of a paring knife. Add the monkfish, cod, swordfish, and parsley. Stir gently to combine. Simmer until the fish has just turned opaque, about 4 minutes. Add the clams and cook gently until they have opened, about 5 minutes, depending upon the freshness of the clams. Taste, and adjust seasonings as needed. Serve immediately and very hot in shallow bowls, with rouille (below) and a basket of croutons.

ROUILLE
Garlic Saffron Mayonnaise
(MAKES ABOUT 1 CUP)

The French word rouille *means "rust," and this super-pungent, slightly hot sauce is so named for its rusty sunset–like hue. Its base is a mayonnaise, which actually takes only minutes to make with the help of a food processor. If you want, you can substitute a best-quality commercial brand mayonnaise, but the end results would be like comparing average to amazing. This rouille recipe uses just half of the total mayonnaise recipe. Refrigerate the rest for up to a few days.*

For the mayonnaise base:

1 tablespoon Dijon mustard

1 whole egg

2 egg yolks

1 tablespoon fresh lemon juice

1 teaspoon salt

Generous pinch of ground white pepper

1 1/2 cups vegetable, peanut, or canola oil

1/2 cup extra virgin olive oil

To finish the rouille

8 saffron threads, crumbled between fingers

3 cloves garlic, finely chopped and smashed into a
    paste

1/4 cup very finely chopped jarred pimento

1 teaspoon fresh lemon juice

1/2 teaspoon red chili pepper flakes

Pinch of paprika

Salt and ground white pepper

In a food processor with a plastic blade (or a blender), pulse together the mustard, whole egg, egg yolks, lemon juice, salt, and pepper until frothy, about 20 to 25 pulses. Combine the oils in a large measuring cup with a lip for pouring. Then, with the processor motor still running, very slowly dribble in small amounts of oil. Continue until you've added about 3/4 cup of oil. The emulsification (or "coming together") should begin at this point, and the mayonnaise will change from liquid to slightly thick. Add the remaining oil in a steadier stream now, until it is gone. Voila—mayonnaise! Taste, and adjust seasonings. Remove all but 1 cup from the processor and refrigerate in a sealed nonreactive plastic or glass container.

To finish the rouille, add to the 1 cup mayonnaise remaining in the food processor all the rouille ingredients except the salt and pepper. Process all of the ingredients together until airy and smooth, about 1 minute, just long enough to blend in the seasonings. Taste, and adjust seasonings as needed. Cover and refrigerate until ready to use.

PERNOD AND PASTIS

Pernod Fils and Pernod-Ricard are both popular brands of the anise-flavored liqueur pastis. Though frequently associated with Provence, Pernod is consumed all over France as a beverage, served over ice. Its taste is milky and sweet. Pernod is integral to Bouillabaisse and Soupe de Poisson. Keep some in your liquor cabinet to bring instant licorice flavor to almost anything you're cooking. Small doses are better, as the flavor is strong.

SOUPE DE POISSON
Fish Soup
(MAKES 8 TO 10 SERVINGS)

Another quintessential fish soup, fragrant Soupe de Poisson hails from the coastal communities of Southern France. Variations of this chunky soup are ubiquitous in the colorful, blue-awning-lined bistros that are like so many boats bobbing in the Mediterranean Sea. Soupe de Poisson is similar to Bouillabaisse in that it utilizes fennel, saffron, and a few other shared ingredients, and it is also garnished with rouille and croutons. Except here, the croutons are topped with grated Gruyère cheese and dunked into the soup. Another significant difference is that it is partially puréed, unlike Bouillabaisse, where all the parts are kept separate and whole. Because the fish is chunky, it is tough to break it up properly with an immersion blender. Instead, I suggest puréeing half in a traditional blender and then returning it to the remaining, un-puréed soup.

3 tablespoons olive oil

1 medium onion, finely chopped

2 leeks, trimmed 1 inch above the white part, halved vertically, well rinsed, and finely chopped

1 fennel bulb, (stems and fronds removed and reserved), halved, cored, and finely chopped

Salt and freshly ground black pepper

4 large cloves garlic, smashed and coarsely chopped

4 large ripe Roma tomatoes, coarsely chopped

1 tablespoon tomato paste

1/4 cup plus 2 tablespoons Pernod

1 cup Chardonnay or another good-quality, full-bodied white wine

2 tablespoons fresh orange juice

5 saffron threads

1 teaspoon dried tarragon

Pinch of crushed red pepper

2 bay leaves

4 cups Fish Stock (see page 17)

1 pound cod, boned and cut into 1-inch chunks

1 pound grouper, boned and cut into 1-inch chunks

1/2 pound shelled, deveined shrimp, coarsely chopped

Garnish:

Croutons (see page 41)

Rouille (see page 42)

1/2 cup grated Gruyère cheese

1/4 cup reserved fennel fronds, finely chopped

In a 5 1/2-quart Dutch oven or similarly sized pot, heat the olive oil over medium heat. Add the onion, leeks, and fennel bulb, and season lightly with salt and pepper. Stir and cook for 5 minutes, or until just softened. Add the garlic, tomatoes, and tomato paste. Stir to coat, and cook through over medium-high heat for 1 to 2 minutes. Add the Pernod and reduce down to a glaze. Add the Chardonnay and reduce by half. Add orange juice, saffron, and tarragon, then season lightly again with salt and pepper. Stir to coat. Add the crushed red pepper, bay leaves, and fumet. Bring to a boil over high heat; reduce to a simmer and cook uncovered for 25 minutes, skimming off any foam as you go. Add the cod and grouper. Poach gently at a low simmer until the fish becomes opaque and starts to flake, about 10 minutes. Add the shrimp and cook for another 2 minutes. Remove the bay leaves.

To finish, purée half the soup in a blender until smooth, using equal parts liquid and solids. Return the purée to the pot. Taste, and adjust seasonings as needed. (*Note*: The soup can be stored in the refrigerator for a day or two.)

To serve, heat the soup thoroughly. Serve in individual bowls or a tureen, with rouille, croutons, and Gruyère. Each serving should be topped with a crouton and a generous dollop of rouille and drizzled with Gruyère. Sprinkle a dusting of bright green fennel fronds over the top if desired.

THE NITTY-GRITTY ON LEEKS

Because they grow from the ground up, the tightly bound leaves of this mildly onion-flavored vegetable tend to attract and hold onto dirt as they grow. It is very important to get all of the dirt out to prevent unseemly, gritty food. The best way to do that is to cut off the deep green tops down to about 1 inch above where they meet the white end of the leek tubes. (These greens are too tough for most recipes but are wonderful additions to stocks. Set them aside, give them a good soak in a bowl of cold water, and then remove and freeze for later use.)

To clean the edible white and light green portion of the leeks, trim and discard the hairy base and cut the leeks into whatever size the recipe calls for. Then submerge the cut leeks in a large bowl of cool, clean water. The dirt will fall to the bottom. Swish the leeks vigorously, remove them from the bowl, change the washing water, and repeat until the water in the bowl is completely clear and grit free. It usually takes 2 to 3 passes but is well worth the investment of time and energy to enjoy the flavor that leeks impart.

LE-JOUR-APRÈS-NOËL
SOUPE À LA DINDE
The Day-After-Christmas Turkey Soup

(MAKES 6 TO 8 SERVINGS)

In France, goose and duck tend to make the Christmas celebration menu. These are often roasted along with chestnuts (marrons). *However, because turkey tends to steal the holiday show in the States, I wanted to show how a turkey carcass and leftover vegetables can be put to use in this elegant, light soup, sprinkled with a tiny dice of vegetables and rich crimini mushrooms. Here, it is finished with petite croutons, but feel free to stir in ¹/4 cup or so of finely chopped canned chestnuts to give it even more French holiday flair. Make the stock the night after the meal is finished, and this soup comes together quickly the next day. If you have leftover roast turkey, add as suggested. If not, the soup is delicious without meat.*

1 tablespoon unsalted butter

1 tablespoon olive oil

1 medium onion, chopped into a brunoise
  (see page 52)

2 large ribs celery, chopped into a brunoise

2 large carrots, peeled and chopped into a brunoise

2 cloves garlic, smashed and very finely chopped

Salt and freshly ground black pepper

2 cups very finely chopped crimini mushrooms,
  tough stems removed first

1¹/4 teaspoons dried rubbed or ground sage

¹/4 cup dry vermouth

6 cups Turkey Stock (see page 18)

2 cups ¹/4-inch-cubed turkey breast (optional)

For the croutons:

1 tablespoon unsalted butter

1 tablespoon olive oil

1 cup day-old French baguette bread cut into a
  brunoise

¹/2 teaspoon dried rubbed or ground sage

Salt and freshly ground black pepper

Garnish:

1 tablespoon fresh rosemary leaves, finely chopped

In a 5¹/2-quart Dutch oven or similarly sized pot, melt together the butter and olive oil over medium heat. Add the onion, celery, carrots, garlic, and a light sprinkling of salt and pepper. Stir to coat. Reduce heat to medium-low. Cook the vegetables until just softened, about 5 minutes, stirring once or twice. Add the chopped mushrooms (see How to Clean Mushrooms, facing) and sage; stir. Cook for 2 minutes to soften. Add the vermouth, increase heat to medium-high, and cook off the vermouth until almost a glaze, 3 to 5 minutes. Add the stock and turkey. Bring to a boil and reduce to a simmer uncovered over medium heat for 10 to 15 minutes. Taste carefully and

adjust seasonings as needed. If desired, finish with a splash of vermouth.

To prepare the croutons, melt the butter and olive oil together in a medium sauté pan over medium heat. Add the bread, sage, and salt and pepper to taste. Toss to coat. Cook over medium heat until golden, about 3 minutes. Turn out onto paper towels to drain.

Serve the soup in shallow bowls, garnishing each with a small mound of croutons in the center and a sprinkling of fresh rosemary.

HOW TO CLEAN MUSHROOMS

All fresh mushrooms are extremely porous—virtual vegetable sponges. So, with the exception of morels (which are less porous and trap a lot of dirt in their gills), they should not be submerged in water for cleaning. Instead, trim off the often dirty base at the foot of the mushroom stems. If the stems are very tough, gently pull them out of the mushroom and discard or freeze for later use in a vegetable stock. The mushroom head simply needs to be gently brushed with a damp paper towel to remove any dirt. Be sure to clean your work surface thoroughly before chopping the cleaned mushrooms.

CHAPTER 3

LES SOUPES FROIDES
Chilled Soups

France's celebrated crystalline sunlight, particularly in the South of France during arid, hot summer months, calls for shade, simplicity, and a bowl of cooling soup. The exquisite soups on the following pages are mostly created with hot-weather produce, including tomatoes, peppers, cucumbers, and cantaloupe. All are delicious cold, and a few, including Garlicky Vichyssoise with Parsley Oil (page 58), Roasted Tomato Soup with Croutons and Bacon (page 53), and Purely Pepper Soup (page 55), are also delicious hot.

There is really nothing complicated about cold soups, but there are a few tricks to keep in mind. First, chilling anything weakens seasoning, particularly salt and pepper. It is crucial to taste the soup after it is chilled, and adjust seasonings as needed before serving. (Also, just as hot soups must be served very hot, cold soups must be served chilled.) As always, pay attention to garnishes and presentation. Looks count as much as taste, particularly with delicate, cold soups.

Soupe de Concombre et du Fenouil aux Crevettes
Chilled Cucumber and Fennel Soup with Shrimp

(MAKES 4 TO 6 SERVINGS)

Fragrant, delicate cucumbers make fantastic soup-fellows with mildly licorice-scented fennel. Both ingredients are products of hot summer months. Here the cucumbers are puréed until frothy and finished with tiny bites of fresh fennel (see Brunoise Basics, page 52), sour cream, a crowning of fresh herbs, and Provence's reigning liqueur, Pernod. Once chilled, finely chopped seared shrimp give a simultaneous blush of pink color and complementary flavor. This is an exceptionally beautiful, almost feminine, soup, especially with the flirtatious finish of finely chopped fennel fronds and sweet, briny shrimp. Because of the delicate flavors and milky color of the soup, I recommend using white ground pepper, but black pepper will work fine in a pinch.

4 medium cucumbers, peeled, halved, seeded, and cut into 1/4-inch-thick slices (about 6 cups)

1 tablespoon salt, plus more to taste

1/2 medium yellow onion, coarsely chopped (about 3/4 cup)

1 cup whole sour cream

3 tablespoons water

Salt and ground white pepper

1 medium fennel bulb, halved, cored, and cut into a brunoise (about 1 1/2 cups); fronds reserved, stems discarded

2 tablespoons finely chopped reserved fennel fronds

2 tablespoons chopped chives

1/2 teaspoon Pernod or another anise-flavored liqueur

For the shrimp garnish:

1 tablespoon olive oil

1/2 pound medium-size (16-20 count) raw shrimp, shelled and deveined

Salt and ground white pepper

Chopped reserved fennel fronds, for garnish

Toss the cucumbers with 1 tablespoon salt and place in a colander in your kitchen sink to degorge, (draw out excess water) for 30 minutes. Then rinse the cucumbers very well under cold running water. Press them firmly between your palms to extract most of the remaining water from the cucumbers. They will have reduced in size by about one-third. Place the cucumbers in a blender or a food processor fitted with a metal blade, along with the onion, sour cream, and water. Process until frothy and smooth. Turn out into a medium bowl. Season to taste with salt and pepper. Fold in the fennel brunoise, chopped fennel fronds, chives, and Pernod. Cover and chill for at least 30 minutes.

Meanwhile, for the shrimp garnish, heat the olive oil in a medium skillet over medium-high heat. Add the shrimp after about 30 seconds, seasoning lightly with salt and pepper. Turn after

continued >

1 minute, and cook the second side 1 minute, or until the shrimp are slightly golden on the outside and opaque in the center. When cool enough to handle, chop finely.

To finish, taste, and adjust seasonings in the chilled soup before serving. Ladle the chilled soup into shallow bowls and place a small pyramid of chopped shrimp in the center. Garnish with a sprinkling of chopped fennel fronds.

Variations: Use browned chopped bacon or thin strips of Prosciutto or another ham as a substitute for shrimp.

BRUNOISE BASICS

Any vegetable can be chopped into a brunoise, which is essentially a tiny dice of approximately ¼-inch-thick cubes. Most commonly, a brunoise is used when "petite" is in order for a garnish (as in the cucumber soup for the fennel and shrimp garnish), or for fast, even cooking (as with the croutons in the Roasted Tomato Soup, facing).

The way things are cut depends largely on the shape of the vegetable or product. For example, with the fennel in the previous soup, the bulb itself is cut in half vertically. Then each half is cut into thin vertical strips (after removing the tough central core). These are bundled into neat stacks, turned a quarter turn, and the strips are then finely chopped into a dice, or brunoise. The process is very similar for cucumbers, peppers, zucchini, carrots, and vegetables of many other shapes and sizes. It helps to have a very sharp chef's knife, but be careful to keep your fingertips curved in as you chop to avoid cutting yourself.

Soupe aux Tomates au Four avec Croûtons et Lardons
Roasted Tomato Soup with Croutons and Bacon

(MAKES 4 TO 6 SERVINGS)

Roasting year-round grape tomatoes makes these already sweet gems an even sweeter backdrop for fresh thyme-cloaked croutons and salty bacon. A swirl of crème fraîche on top delivers a crowning French flavor twist.

4 cups fresh red grape tomatoes

1 large shallot, cut into 8 pieces

1 teaspoon Champagne vinegar or cider vinegar

1 teaspoon extra virgin olive oil

Salt and freshly ground black pepper

4 sprigs fresh thyme

1 cup Chicken Stock (see page 18)

For the croutons:

1/2 small day-old baguette, cut into 1/4-inch cubes

1 tablespoon finely chopped fresh thyme leaves

2 tablespoons olive oil

Salt and freshly ground black pepper

To garnish:

1/4 cup Crème Fraîche (see page 54)

4 slices bacon, browned, drained, and coarsely chopped (optional)

1 tablespoon chopped fresh thyme leaves

Preheat oven to 450 degrees F.

In a roasting pan or full-sized rimmed baking sheet, combine the tomatoes, shallot, vinegar, and olive oil, tossing to coat evenly. Season lightly with salt and pepper. Top with the fresh thyme sprigs. Roast for about 30 minutes, or until the tomatoes start to pop and implode, tossing 15 minutes into the cooking time. Remove tomatoes and leave the oven on (for the croutons). Discard the thyme branches.

Spoon the roasted tomatoes, shallot, and any juices into a food processor fitted with a metal blade or a blender. Use the chicken stock to deglaze the hot roasting pan, stirring up any browned bits, then add the stock to the processor or blender. Blend until chunky smooth. Season to taste with salt and pepper. Turn into a bowl, cover, and chill for at least 3 hours or overnight.

To make the croutons, in a medium bowl, toss together the bread cubes, thyme, olive oil, and salt and pepper to taste. Turn out onto a small baking sheet and roast in the preheated 450-degree-F oven until golden brown, about 15 to 20 minutes, tossing once. Set aside to cool.

To serve, ladle the soup into individual bowls, top each with a dollop of crème fraîche, 4 or 5 croutons, 1/2 teaspoon bacon, and a sprinkling of fresh thyme leaves.

CRÈME FRAÎCHE

MAKES 1 CUP

Crème Fraîche, a thick, fermented whole cream, is the darling of Dieppe, in the milk and apple rich region of Normandy, France. Though finding it in the United States is increasingly easier, it can still be a challenge. For a more authentic and easier crème fraîche, it is best to make your own. In addition to its distinctive creamy flavor, crème fraîche (made with heavy cream) will not break when cooked into soups or sauces and makes a beautiful garnish for any soup, hot or cold. Making it is in a snap.

1 cup heavy cream   1 tablespoon plain yogurt or buttermilk

Combine cream with yogurt or buttermilk in a lidded glass jar or plastic container. Shake vigorously to combine. Leave out at room temperature, covered, until the mixture starts to thicken, 12 to 24 hours. Refrigerate for up to 2 weeks, until ready to use. The longer it is stored, the more tangy it becomes.

PUREMENT POIVRON SOUPE
Purely Pepper Soup

(MAKES 4 TO 6 SERVINGS)

Like Roasted Tomato Soup (see page 53) this "belle" soup gets its sweet flavor cues from roasting, enhanced here with a splash of sweet and sassy sherry vinegar and a pinch of heat from red chili flakes. The ingredients and flavors recall warm, sunny southern France, particularly Provence and Catalan, near the border of northern Spain. In this exquisite soup, the roasting also serves the purpose of loosening the pepper skins for removal. Use a blend of sweet bell pepper colors, but avoid green, since they are too bitter for this soup, which is also magnificent served hot in cooler months.

For roasting:

5 sweet bell peppers (combine orange, yellow, and red, if possible), trimmed, halved, and seeded

1 tablespoon olive oil

For the soup base:

1 tablespoon extra virgin olive oil

1 medium onion, finely chopped

Salt and freshly ground black pepper

Generous pinch of red chili pepper flakes

$^1/_2$ teaspoon sherry vinegar

4 cups vegetable stock or water

3 tablespoons basmati rice

$^1/_4$ cup Crème Fraîche (see facing page), for garnish

Preheat broiler to high.

Toss the prepared peppers with the olive oil in a rimmed sheet pan or a roasting pan. Arrange in a single layer, skin side up. Place in the oven on the highest rack near the broiler. Broil for 10 to 15 minutes, or until the skins start to bubble and char. Remove from the oven, move to a medium bowl, and cover tightly with plastic wrap. Steam the peppers for 10 to 15 minutes to loosen the skins.

Meanwhile, in a 5$^1/_2$-quart Dutch oven or a similarly sized soup pot, heat 1 tablespoon olive oil over medium heat. Add the onion and a bit of salt and pepper. Stir to coat. Cook for 3 minutes to soften. Add the chili pepper flakes and sweat together for another 5 minutes.

From the steamed peppers, remove any charred or loosened skin and discard. Turn out all of the peppers and their juices into the soup base. Increase heat to medium-high. Deglaze the soup pot with the vinegar, stirring to pick up any bits. Add the vegetable stock or water, rice, and a generous dash of salt and pepper. Bring to a boil over high heat, then reduce to a simmer over medium-low heat. Cook for 25 minutes, or until the rice is soft. Purée with a blender or food processor fitted with a metal blade until smooth. Taste, and adjust seasonings as needed. Pour into a large bowl, cover with plastic wrap, and refrigerate at least 3 hours or overnight.

Serve very cold in attractive bowls with a dollop of crème fraîche.

SOUPE AU CANTALOUP ET AU CHAMPAGNE AVEC PROSCIUTTO ET BASILIC

Cantaloupe and Champagne Soup with Prosciutto and Basil

(MAKES 4 TO 6 SERVINGS)

When I lived in south-central France, a combination of deep orange melon slices wrapped with see-through slivers of salty, dry-cured ham served with cold, sparkling Blanquette de Limoux were de rigueur *starts to most summer evenings. This super refreshing soup is a delightful play on these flavor themes with added counterpoints of black pepper and fresh basil. I use the best-quality Brut Champagne I can afford instead of Blanquette (which is hard to find in the States, but not impossible), and use the best-quality dry-cured ham available, whether it be prosciutto, Jambon de Parme, or Jambon Sec. Serve icy cold and while the bubbly is still bubbling. The addition of a small amount of cream recalls a kind of soup sorbet.*

$^1/_2$ large, ripe cantaloupe, seeded, peeled, and cut
    into 1-inch cubes
$^2/_3$ cup Brut Champagne
$^1/_2$ cup whole cream
Salt and freshly ground black pepper
Zest of 1 lime

For garnish:

8 slices prosciutto or another dry-cured ham,
    julienned or sliced into thin ribbons
1 tablespoon chopped fresh basil leaves
1 teaspoon extra virgin olive oil

In a blender or the bowl of a food processor fitted with a metal blade, combine the cantaloupe, Champagne, and whole cream (do not substitute a lighter cream). Pulse to blend until frothy and smooth. Pour into a medium bowl. Season to taste with salt and pepper. Stir in lime zest. Cover and chill for 1 to 2 hours.

    Serve in shallow bowls. Pile a small mound of ham in the center of each bowl, and garnish with a bit of fresh basil and a few drops of olive oil. Serve immediately and very cold.

VICHYSSOISE À L'AIL ET À L'HUILE DU PERSIL
Garlicky Vichyssoise with Parsley Oil
(MAKES 6 TO 8 SERVINGS)

This creamy, airy blend of leeks, onion, potatoes, cream, and chicken stock gets taken to a new, sweeter level with the addition of roasted garlic. This classic soup was likely created and named in the United States by French chef Louis Diat, of New York's Ritz Carlton, who named it after Vichy, France, near his hometown. Typically served cold, it is also magnificent hot. Either way, fresh parsley oil adds a swath of emerald color and a mild, grassy flavor to each spoonful. Make it a day ahead, and the flavors will deepen even more.

1 head garlic

3 tablespoons extra virgin olive oil, plus 1 teaspoon
    for drizzling

1 medium onion, coarsely chopped

Salt and freshly ground black pepper

6 medium leeks, trimmed to about 1 inch above the
    white part, cut into 1-inch lengths and washed
    (see The Nitty-Gritty on Leeks, page 45)

3 medium Yukon Gold potatoes, peeled, and cut into
    2-inch cubes

4 cups Chicken Stock (see page 18)

1 teaspoon dried thyme

1 teaspoon dry vermouth

1 cup half & half

Parsley Oil (see facing page)

Preheat the oven to 425 degrees F.

    Cut off the papery top of the garlic head and drizzle with about 1 teaspoon olive oil. Wrap with aluminum foil into a ball, twisting the top tightly. Roast until softened, about 45 minutes. Remove from the oven to cool.

    Meanwhile, heat the 3 tablespoons olive oil in a 5 1/2-quart Dutch oven or sturdy soup pot over medium heat. Add the onion and season lightly with salt and pepper; cook to soften, about 3 minutes. Add the leeks and another dash of salt and pepper; stir. Cook over medium heat for 10 minutes, or until softened. Add the potatoes, chicken stock, and thyme. Bring to a boil over high heat, then reduce to a simmer over medium-low heat. Cover and cook for 30 minutes, or until the potatoes and leeks are very tender.

    Remove the foil from around the cooled garlic and squeeze the entire head between your index finger and thumb to extract the cooked flesh. Discard the papery casings and add the garlic to the soup. Using a blender or food processor fitted with a metal blade, blend the soup until it is very smooth and airy and free of potato chunks. Add the vermouth and half & half. Whisk to blend.

Taste and carefully adjust seasonings with salt and pepper. Chill thoroughly, covered, for at least 3 hours or overnight. (*Note:* Soup can be kept in the refrigerator for up to 2 days.)

Serve either very cold or very hot, with a swirl of parsley oil (below) on the top of each bowl.

Garnish Variations: Bacon, thyme croutons (see page 53), fresh thyme, or crème fraîche (see page 54) would pair beautifully with this soup.

L'Huile du Persil
Parsley Oil
(MAKES ABOUT 1¼ CUPS)

It is possible to make an herb-flavored oil with just about any herb—basil, rosemary, and thyme all come to mind as outstanding substitutes and all are used liberally in French kitchens. Parsley is particularly durable and colorful. This oil will last for up to a week, covered in the refrigerator. Its bright green hue is an exceptional complement to the milky, pale green of Vichyssoise, and it is nutritious, to boot. Drizzle any leftovers over greens and incorporate into vinaigrettes for added panache.

1 bunch fresh parsley (flat or curly leaf), stems removed

1 cup extra virgin olive oil

Rinse the parsley thoroughly under running cold water. Drain in a colander. Squeeze out any excess water using your hands. Place in the bowl of a food processor fitted with a metal blade, and add the olive oil. Process until very smooth. Pour out into a medium bowl, cover, and allow to steep for 30 minutes to 1 hour.

In batches, strain the mixture into the mouth of a clean Mason jar or other container passing through a very fine cheesecloth or two paper coffee filters stacked upon each other. As the oil starts to slowly move through the filters, squeeze gently with your hand to help release all of the flavored oil into the container, being careful not to break the filters. (If that happens, replace with new ones.) Continue until all of the oil has been strained. Discard the parsley solids. Seal or cover and refrigerate the oil until ready to use. Bring to room temperature before using.

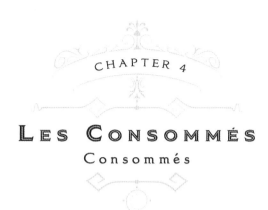

CHAPTER 4

LES CONSOMMÉS
Consommés

Consommé is the consummate soup. A darling of the Belle Époque in nineteenth-century France and elsewhere, it is a dainty soup that deserves to be served in pretty, petite bowls and demands polite sipping. Made from stocks that are clarified with egg whites and enriched with meat (or seafood) and vegetables, consommés become as clear as the Azure Sea and can be finished with anything from fresh herbs to pasta, truffles, and even savory cream puffs.

It's a shame that consommés have slipped somewhat out of fashion, because they are truly a pleasure to look at and eat. Extra bonuses: they can be made ahead and are quite versatile. The process of making a consommé is not complicated, but it takes a little time. Make a good homemade stock several days ahead and freeze it to break up the work.

Once the stock is at room temperature, combine with a mixture of egg whites, sometimes ground meat, and finely minced vegetables. These ingredients do two things: they add a second, corresponding level of flavor to the soup and, most importantly, the egg whites clarify the stock, literally pulling out impurities as the strange-looking mixture simmers along.

For about the first 15 minutes, the egg/meat/vegetable mixture needs to be stirred basically nonstop with a wooden spoon, to make sure none of the crucial egg whites stick to the bottom or sides. After that, it is left alone uncovered, and the most miraculous thing happens: the mixture starts cooking and thickening at the top and becomes what is known in consommé circles as a "draft." After 30 minutes, the rather ugly draft has done its work and what lies below is a beautiful, clear consommé.

Next, a ladle is nudged into the draft to form an opening, and the consommé is ladled through a fine sieve lined with three paper towels into a waiting bowl. The draft is then discarded.

After that, the list is virtually endless on ways to finish the seasoning and garnishes for the consommé, but they should be petite, pretty, and pair with the flavor of the stock. Nothing clunky will do. This chapter gives you an opportunity to pull out your food processor, which does an excellent job of mincing the vegetables finely for the clarifying mixture. All consommés can be prepared ahead and frozen or refrigerated, but add the garnishes just before serving the steaming soup, preferably in your prettiest dishes or cups.

Consommé de Bœuf aux Champignons et à la Ciboulette

Beef Consommé with Mushrooms and Chives

(MAKES 4 TO 6 SERVINGS)

Whisper-thin slices of button mushrooms are added to the hot, nearly finished consommé to cook just five minutes. The "feet" of the mushrooms that have been removed from the caps are added to the vegetable mixture for another layer of flavor. Finished with a sprinkle of fresh, green chives, this is an excellent consommé for beginners, as it relatively simple to make and simply beautiful to behold.

2 ribs celery, chopped into 2-inch lengths

1 leek, trimmed 1 inch above the white root, halved
    vertically, well rinsed, and cut into 2-inch lengths

14 button mushrooms, cleaned and feet separated
    from caps (see How to Clean Mushrooms,
    page 47), caps reserved

1 medium onion, quartered

1/4 cup chopped fresh parsley leaves and stems

4 egg whites

1/2 pound lean ground beef

1 teaspoon salt

10 black peppercorns, lightly cracked using a
    chef's knife

6 cups best-quality beef stock (see page 15),
    room temperature

To finish the soup:

1 tablespoon cognac

4 cups very thinly sliced reserved mushrooms

Salt and freshly ground black pepper

2 tablespoons finely chopped chives

Place the celery, leek, mushroom feet, onion, and parsley in the bowl of a food processor fitted with a metal blade. Pulse until very fine, about 30 seconds. Set aside.

Place the egg whites in a very large bowl and whisk energetically with a whisk until frothy, about 1 minute. Whisk the reserved vegetable mixture into the egg whites and combine. Fold in the ground beef, salt, and peppercorns with a wooden spoon and stir to combine.

Place the stock in a 5 1/2-quart Dutch oven or similarly sized pot. Stir in the vegetable/beef/ egg white mixture with a wooden spoon. Turn on heat to medium, and cook uncovered, stirring constantly, until the stock comes to a simmer, about 15 minutes. The draft will now form. Stop stirring and allow to simmer for 30 minutes, making sure to keep it at a low simmer to keep the draft intact. Meanwhile, line a sieve with three paper towels and set it inside a large bowl.

Remove the pot from the heat. Gently break a hole in the draft with the bottom of a ladle, and start scooping the consommé through the sieve and into the bowl. Keep working until only the draft remains in the pot. Discard the draft. The consommé can be refrigerated or frozen at this point.

To finish, heat the consommé over medium-high heat in a medium saucepan until simmering. Add the cognac and mushrooms. Taste, and adjust seasoning. Cook for 3 to 5 minutes, or until the mushrooms are just wilted. Serve with a sprinkle of fresh chives, being sure to get mushrooms in every bowl.

Variations: Another way to use a good beef stock consommé such as this is to serve it with a combination of julienned vegetables, such as carrot, turnip, leek, celery, onion, and cabbage. After cutting the vegetables into julienne, simmer them in the warm consommé just before serving. They add extra delicious flavor at the last minute and are also beautiful.

CONSOMMÉ DE VOLAILLE AU POULET POCHÉ ET AUX POIS FRAIS
Consommé with Poached Chicken and Fresh Peas

(MAKES 6 SERVINGS)

This chicken stock–based consommé is exceptionally delicate and reminiscent of spring, with the bright, sweet green peas and fresh tarragon garnish. The chicken breast needs to be cut into thin "threads" to keep things very refined. The best way to do this is to cut the breast vertically into several ¼-inch-thick pieces, stack those, and then cut through horizontally at ¼-inch thickness. The chicken needs to be poached separately from the consommé, as it will muddle the clarity of the consommé to poach it in the clarified stock.

1 leek, trimmed to 1 inch above the white root, halved vertically, well rinsed, and cut into 2-inch lengths

2 medium carrots, peeled and cut into 2-inch lengths

2 ribs celery, cut into 2-inch lengths

1 medium onion, quartered

2 cloves garlic

¼ cup fresh parsley leaves and stems

4 egg whites

½ pound ground chicken

1 teaspoon salt

8 cups homemade Chicken Stock (see page 18), or best-quality commercial brand chicken stock, room temperature

1 (1-pound) boneless, skinless chicken breast cut into very thin ¼-inch-thick strips

1 teaspoon salt

Salt and freshly ground black pepper

1 cup fresh or frozen peas

1 teaspoon fresh tarragon leaves

Place the leek, carrots, celery, onion, garlic, and parsley in the bowl of a food processor fitted with a metal blade. Pulse until very fine, about 30 seconds. Set aside. Place the egg whites in a very large bowl and whisk energetically with a whisk until frothy, about 1 minute. Whisk the reserved vegetable mixture into the egg whites and combine. Fold in the ground chicken and salt with a wooden spoon, and stir to combine.

Place the room-temperature stock in a 5½-quart Dutch oven or similarly sized pot. Stir in the vegetable/chicken/egg white mixture with a wooden spoon. Turn on heat to medium, and cook uncovered, stirring constantly, until the stock comes to a simmer, about 15 minutes. The draft will now form. Stop stirring and allow to simmer for 30 minutes, making sure to keep it at a low simmer to keep the draft intact. Meanwhile, line a sieve with three paper towels and set it inside a large bowl.

Remove pot from the heat. Gently break a hole in the draft with the bottom of a ladle, and start scooping the consommé through the sieve and into the bowl. Keep working until all that is left in the pot is the draft. Discard the draft. The consommé can be refrigerated or frozen at this point.

To finish, in a medium skillet over medium heat, place the sliced chicken in just enough water to cover. Add the salt and cook until chicken is opaque in the center, about 3 minutes. Strain out the liquid and set aside.

Heat the consommé over medium-high heat in a medium saucepan until simmering. Just before serving, taste, and adjust seasonings, and add peas to the consommé. Cook just until softened but still brilliant green, about 3 minutes. Place a small mound of chicken in the bottom of each bowl, and then ladle the hot consommé on top. Garnish with several tarragon leaves. Serve immediately.

CONSOMMÉ DE TOMATES AUX CREVETTES ET AUX FENOUIL
Tomato Consommé with Shrimp and Fennel
(MAKES 6 TO 8 SERVINGS)

The clarification process renders the tomato-infused fish stock a spectacular pale yellow hue. Fresh grape tomatoes pop with each bite, and the pretty fennel fronds finish the dish off beautifully. The clarified base can be made ahead and the garnishes added at the bottom of each bowl at the last minute, before ladling the hot, clarified broth over the top.

¹/₄ pound medium-size (16-20 count) shell-on raw
   shrimp
1 onion, quartered
1 fennel bulb, cored and cut into 8 large chunks
   (reserve fronds for garnish)
¹/₄ cup fresh tarragon stems and leaves
3 cloves garlic
2 cups San Marzano canned whole tomatoes or
   another plum tomato, with juice
4 egg whites
1 teaspoon salt

10 peppercorns, crushed
6 cups homemade Fish Stock (see page 17)
   or best-quality commercial brand fish stock,
   room temperature
Salt and freshly ground black pepper

For the garnish:

Reserved shrimp
Salt
1 cup grape tomatoes, halved vertically
¹/₄ cup reserved fennel fronds

To devein the shrimp, cut through their arched backs about ¹/₈ inch with kitchen shears. Pull off the shells and tails; rinse and reserve. Remove any veins and rinse the shrimp well under cold water. Reserve shrimp in fridge.

In the bowl of a food processor fitted with a metal blade, pulse together the shrimp shells and tails, onion, fennel bulb, tarragon, garlic, and tomatoes with juices, until fine, about 30 seconds. Set aside. In a large bowl, energetically whisk together the egg whites, salt, and peppercorns for 1 minute, until very frothy. Whisk the reserved vegetable/shrimp base into the egg whites.

Pour the fish stock into a 5¹/₂-quart Dutch oven or similarly sized pot. Stir in the vegetable/shrimp/egg white mixture with a wooden spoon. Turn on heat to medium, and cook uncovered, stirring constantly, until the stock comes to a simmer, about 15 minutes. The draft will now form. Stop stirring and allow to simmer for 30 minutes, making sure to keep it at a low simmer to keep the draft intact. Meanwhile, line a sieve with three paper towels and set it inside a large bowl.

Remove the pot from the heat. Gently break a hole in the draft with the bottom of a ladle, and start scooping the consommé through the sieve and into the bowl. Keep working until all that is left in the pot is the draft. Discard the draft. The consommé can be refrigerated or frozen at this point. Taste, and adjust seasonings carefully.

Just before serving, prepare the garnishes. Place the shrimp in a small skillet with just enough water to cover halfway, season with a generous pinch of salt, and simmer over medium-high heat. Cook until just opaque, about 2 minutes for medium (16 to 20-count) shrimp. Remove the shrimp from the water with a slotted spoon; when cool enough to handle, cut them neatly in half horizontally. Place 4 or 5 of the halved shrimp in the bottom of shallow bowls. Scatter halved grape tomatoes (about 8) and 2 or 3 fennel fronds over the shrimp. Ladle the hot consommé into each bowl and serve immediately.

Soupe aux Poivrons Rouges
Roasted Pepper Consommé with Ditalini Pasta

(MAKES 6 TO 8 SERVINGS)

This gorgeous consommé combines rich beef stock with sweet roasted peppers. A pretty reddish brown in color, cayenne pepper and sherry vinegar deliver "pop" that is softened by the round tubes of petite ditalini pasta. If you can't find this pasta shape in your grocery store, substitute another small tubular or twisted noodle, or just break off vermicelli into 1-inch lengths and cook to al dente, following package directions. This consommé reminds me of some of the kinds of dishes served in Catalan country in south-central France, which is influenced by Spanish cuisine as well as French. Be sure to cook and reserve the pasta separately and plate at the last minute.

1 onion, quartered

2 ribs celery, cut into 2-inch lengths

2 carrots, peeled and cut into 2-inch lengths

2 cloves garlic

1 cup canned roasted peppers* with their juices
    from a 12-ounce jar of roasted peppers; reserve
    rest for garnish

$1/4$ cup chopped fresh parsley

4 egg whites

1 teaspoon salt

10 peppercorns, crushed

$1/2$ pound lean ground beef

6 cups homemade beef stock (see page 15)
    or best-quality commercial brand, room
    temperature

Garnish:

1 cup uncooked ditalini pasta

$1/4$ teaspoon crushed red pepper

1 teaspoon sherry vinegar

Reserved roasted red peppers (about $1/2$ cup) cut
    into thin strips

Finely chopped fresh chives, optional

Place the onion, celery, carrots, garlic, 1 cup roasted peppers and juices, and parsley in the bowl of a food processor fitted with a metal blade (or a blender). Pulse 30 times, until the contents are finely chopped. Set aside.

In a large bowl, vigorously whisk together the egg whites, salt, and peppercorns until frothy, 1 minute. Whisk the vegetable mixture into the egg whites and stir to combine. Crumble the ground beef into this mixture and stir to combine. Meanwhile, line a sieve with three paper towels and set it inside a large bowl.

Pour the beef stock into a $5^{1}/2$-quart Dutch oven or similarly sized pot. Stir in the vegetable/ beef/egg white mixture with a wooden spoon. Turn on heat to medium, and cook uncovered, stirring constantly, until the stock comes to a simmer, about 15 minutes. The draft will now form.

Stop stirring and allow to simmer 30 minutes, making sure to keep it at a low simmer to keep the draft intact.

Remove the pot from the heat. Gently break a hole in the draft with the bottom of a ladle, and start scooping the consommé through the sieve and into the large bowl. Keep working until all that is left in the pot is the draft. Discard the draft. The consommé can be refrigerated or frozen at this point. Taste, and adjust seasonings carefully.

To finish the soup, cook the pasta in well-salted water according to box directions for al dente. Ditalini will take about 10 minutes. Drain and reserve.

Bring the consommé to a simmer. Add the crushed red pepper, vinegar, and reserved red peppers. Taste, and adjust seasonings as needed. Serve the very hot soup ladled over $1/4$ cup of the warm pasta at the bottom of each serving bowl. If desired, garnish with some finely chopped fresh chives.

Alternatively, roast your own peppers (see Purely Pepper Soup, page 55).

CHAPTER 5

LES SOUPES CRÉMEUSES
Creamy Creamed Soups

Here are recipes for luscious soups that will unequivocally put to rest the myth that French creamed soups are laden with fat and starch. Instead, these versions resonate with layered fresh flavors to be sipped delicately from a spoon, not slurped as you would their unseemly canned renditions that really do not belong anywhere except in a circa 1950s American casserole recipe book.

You will notice a refreshingly simple methodology repeated throughout. A stock is built from the trimmings of the principal ingredient(s), and a soup base is separately prepared by sautéing together a few aromatics in butter. This is then sprinkled with flour, which forms a roux. Once the flour is cooked through, the strained fresh broth is returned to the pot, along with the main ingredient (asparagus, mushrooms, onions, etc.) and seasoned with appropriate herbs and wine(s), then briefly cooked to soften the vegetable and marry the flavors. The soup is then puréed (see Immersion Blender Puréeing tips, page 74), finished with a bit of cream, seasoned, and served hot with suggested garnishes.

It is that simple, that delicious, and purely delightful. The method continues the French theme of no-waste cooking—and that's what makes it so wonderful. There is another bonus: all of these soups can be made ahead, but the cream should not be added until just before reheating and serving. *Bon appetit!*

Soupe de Céler-Rave et Celeri
Celery Root and Fresh Celery Soup

(MAKES 8 SERVINGS)

Though a very ugly, knobby-looking food, celery root, or celeriac, is pure elegance in the flavor department and a frequent visitor in French kitchens. Whispers of raw celery flavor run through every bite, balanced by a starchy texture and nutty flavor reminiscent of roasted potatoes. If you can't find it in your market, substitute potatoes and increase the celery ribs from 6 to 8 to increase the lovely, refreshing celery flavor. Like rutabagas and turnips, celery root has a thick double skin. Cut through the skin with a sturdy paring knife and discard it. Be sure to clean up the gritty cutting board before proceeding. The elegance of this soup belies its extremely humble ingredients. Gentler white ground pepper is called for here, to keep everything super delicate and white.

4 tablespoons unsalted butter, divided

1 medium onion, halved and finely diced

6 ribs celery, finely sliced, any feathery leaves reserved

Salt and ground white pepper

3 tablespoons all-purpose flour

2 cups Chicken Stock (see page 18)

2 cups vegetable stock

2 medium-size celery roots, peeled and cut into 1/2-inch cubes (about 3 cups)

1 small Russet potato, peeled and cut into 1/2-inch cubes (about 1 1/2 cups)

1/4 teaspoon celery salt

3 tablespoons heavy cream

1/4 cup finely chopped fresh parsley and/or reserved celery leaves, for garnish

Melt 3 tablespoons of butter in a 5 1/2-quart Dutch oven or similarly sized pot over medium heat. Add the onion and celery and season with salt and white pepper to taste. Stir to coat, and cook for 5 minutes, or until just softened. Sprinkle the flour evenly over the top. Stir to coat, and cook for 1 minute.

Add the chicken stock, vegetable stock, celery root, potato, and celery salt, stirring to incorporate. Bring to a boil over high heat, and then reduce to a simmer over medium-low heat. Once simmering, cook uncovered for 30 to 40 minutes, or until a knife can easily pierce the soft celery root and potato. Process with a blender or food processor until very smooth. Return purée to the pot if you have removed it, and heat through with remaining 1 tablespoon butter and cream. Taste, and adjust seasonings as needed.

Serve hot and garnish each bowl with a flurry of parsley and one or two small celery leaves.

Soupe d'Asperges

Asparagus Soup

(MAKES 6 TO 8 SERVINGS)

A shining example of French method and frugality, this purely asparagus soup uses every part of the tender spring spear and precious little else. A quick asparagus stock is composed using the tougher outer-layer peels and feet. The tender asparagus spears are roasted to intensify flavor and are added near the very end of cooking to maximize color and texture. Leeks provide a bit of oniony brightness, and a tiny splash of cream at the end is the finishing touch for this exquisite, brilliant green, and slightly textured soup.

For the asparagus stock:

2 large bunches (about 40 spears) fresh green
asparagus

1 onion, halved and thinly sliced

2 ribs celery, thinly sliced

7 cups water

1^1/$_2$ teaspoons kosher or sea salt

5 sprigs fresh thyme, bundled together with
kitchen string

For roasting the asparagus:

Reserved, prepped asparagus spears

2 tablespoons extra virgin olive oil

1 teaspoon salt

Generous dash of freshly ground black pepper

To finish:

4 tablespoons unsalted butter

1 shallot, halved and finely chopped

2 leeks, trimmed to 1 inch above the white root
(save the green leaves in the freezer for later use
in a stock), quartered lengthwise, well rinsed,
and finely chopped

Salt and freshly ground black pepper

4 tablespoons all-purpose flour

Reserved roasted asparagus spears, cut into
^{1}/$_4$-inch lengths (put aside ^{1}/$_4$ cup for garnish)

3 tablespoons whipping or heavy cream

1 teaspoon dry vermouth

To make the stock, rinse the asparagus to remove sand. Remove the tough bottom of each spear by cutting about 1 inch off the bottom. Reserve the trimmings in a small bowl. Peel the spears, starting about 1 inch below the tip to the bottom. Reserve the peelings with the feet. Reserve the peeled asparagus separately.

In a 5^1/$_2$-quart Dutch oven or similarly sized pot, combine onion, celery, water, salt, thyme bundle, and asparagus trimmings and peelings. Bring to a boil over high heat, reduce to a mild simmer over medium/medium-low, and cook uncovered for 30 minutes.

continued >

Meanwhile, preheat oven to 450 degrees F. To roast the asparagus, toss the prepped asparagus spears in olive oil, salt, and pepper on a rimmed baking sheet. Then arrange spears in a single layer. Place on the middle oven rack and roast for 20 minutes, or until tender and just starting to take on a little golden color. Toss asparagus midway through cooking. Remove from oven and set aside. When cool enough to handle, cut the tips from 30 asparagus stalks; reserve. Cut the spears into 1/4-inch lengths; reserve.

Strain the finished stock through a China cap or fine colander into a large bowl, pressing against the solids to extract flavor. Discard solids. Keep the strained stock off to the side. Rinse the cooking pot if needed. In the same pot, melt the butter over medium heat, then add the shallot, leeks, and salt and pepper to taste. Stir to coat, and cook for 5 minutes, or until just softened. Sprinkle evenly with the flour and stir to coat. Cook for 1 minute.

Add the reserved stock, stirring. Bring to a boil over high heat, and then reduce to a gentle simmer over medium/medium-low. Cook uncovered for 20 minutes. Remove from the heat.

Purée all the asparagus stalks in the pot with stock or in a stand blender or food processor. Return purée to the pot (if you used a blender or food processor).

Bring it to a low boil over high heat. Stir in the cream and the vermouth. Taste, and adjust seasonings as necessary. Serve the soup very hot. Garnish each bowl with about five spear tips.

IMMERSION BLENDER PURÉEING TIPS

As much as I advocate immersion blenders (which can be used in the same pot as the soup) over traditional blenders (which can seep hot liquid) and food processors (which can do the same and are difficult to clean), there are a few things to consider to ensure a super frothy, smooth purée.

Begin with the blender somewhere near the center of the pot and pressed down nearly all the way to the bottom. Purée on high power for a minute or two. This will create a kind of vortex that will pull the chunky bits into the blender blades. To grab the remaining bigger chunks, lift the blender up, and work it down over them to break them up. This may take a few passes, especially with larger, tougher items, such as stringy celery. Keep going until the soup is the desired consistency. In a creamed soup, I like a very smooth purée, but the occasional chunky bit is just fine. Finish according to recipe directions.

SOUPE "SOUBISE" AUX ECHALOTES FRITES
Onion Soup "Soubise" with Fried Shallots
(MAKES 8 SERVINGS)

A sauce soubise, which I wrote about in The French Cook—Sauces, *is prepared with a béchamel (milk + blond roux) thickened with puréed onions. It is a simply magnificent concoction that goes with everything from pork chops to steak. As a soup, it is essentially the same exact thing, except that the onions are cooked down and sweetened with rich cream, and the soup is later finished with stock, herbs, and more complementary goodness. This is about as delicious a soup as imaginable, and it packs just as much onion flavor as its classic cousin, French Onion Soup (see page 24).*

4 tablespoons unsalted butter

6 medium white onions, halved and thinly sliced
   (about 8 cups)

Salt and freshly ground black pepper

1/3 cup dry vermouth

2 cups heavy cream

5 sprigs fresh thyme, bundled together with
   kitchen string

2 cups vegetable stock, divided

4 tablespoons all-purpose flour

1/2 cup good-quality Chardonnay or another
   white wine

For the fried shallot garnish:

1 tablespoon olive oil

1 large shallot, halved vertically and thinly sliced

Salt and freshly ground black pepper

Melt the butter in a 5 1/2-quart Dutch oven or similarly sized pot over medium heat. Add the onions and a generous dash of salt and pepper. Stir to coat, and, stirring once or twice, cook gently over medium heat for 5 minutes, or until the onions have just started to soften. You do *not* want the onions to brown or take on any color.

Increase heat to high. Add the vermouth and reduce down to nothing, 2 to 3 minutes. Add the cream and fresh thyme bundle. Bring to a boil over high heat and reduce to a simmer over medium/medium-low. Cook uncovered on a low simmer with gentle bubbles until reduced by half and the onions are tender and sweet, stirring occasionally, about 30 minutes. Remove the thyme bundle and discard.

In a small bowl or measuring cup, gradually drizzle 1 cup of the vegetable stock into the flour, whisking as you go to avoid lumps. Pour the mixture (a variation on a "slurry") into the soup pot. Increase heat to high and bring the soup to a boil, stirring. Add the wine, and cook down for 5

in reserved pea and onion stock, green peas, and salt and pepper to taste. Bring to a boil over high heat. Reduce to a simmer over medium/medium-low heat and cook through, 5 to 10 minutes. Remove from heat. Purée until smooth with an immersion blender or food processor. Return to pot (if it has been removed), add cream, and heat through over medium heat for 5 minutes.

To serve, garnish the center of each bowl with a small dollop of crème fraîche or sour cream, sprinkle with a few ribbons of pancetta, and place a fresh mint leaf.

CHAPTER 6

LES BISQUES
Bisques

In the almost ten years I worked as a restaurant critic, I ate more than my fair share of bad bisques. For some reason, this most luscious of classic French soups frequently does not get the attention it deserves. More often than not, it comes out thick enough to throw and stick to a wall like putty and bland enough to dismiss altogether. I suspect the frequent bisque shortfalls have to do with budgetary and technique shortcuts, given that most require fairly expensive seafood ingredients and a little bit of patience.

Happily, with just a little attention to method, bisques are not difficult to make. Perfectly at home as the center of a celebratory meal or special occasion, bisques are creamy, silky soups, with a flavor base made from, or enriched with, crustacean or mollusk shells, including lobster, shrimp, oysters, crabs, and clams. The initial step is to draw the flavor from the shells themselves, usually by steaming them first, sometimes breaking them up with a mallet, and then continuing to cook them into what I call a bisque base, fortified with vegetables, herbs, and usually wine or liqueur. The base is then strained and given a quick purée with a generous dash of cream, and voila—bisque!

The perfect bisque should be liquid enough to easily sip from your spoon, but thick enough to hold its shape in the spoon—almost the same viscosity as wet paint in a can. While rice is a common thickening agent in bisques, I prefer roux for an extra silky texture. Creamed soups made with vegetables or other ingredients are sometimes erroneously deemed bisques. True traditional bisques are all seafood based.

To explain the decadence of beautifully prepared bisque is a difficult thing. Just think heaven (*ciel* in French). It's that close.

Bisque des Crabes Bleus au Thym et au Vermouth
Blue Crab Bisque with Thyme and Vermouth

(MAKES 6 TO 8 SERVINGS)

This recipe is simply sublime! It may seem like a lot of work, but you can do it in three parts: 1) steam the crabs and strain the fumet base; 2) make the bisque base, strain and store overnight in the fridge; 3) finish the bisque in minutes the next day. If you do not have live blue crab, use whatever live sweet crab you can find in your area. If you cannot find any live crab, crush some cooked crab shells (stone crab works) well and simmer them in the same quantity (8 cups) of best-quality fish stock; then proceed according to the directions that follow.

To steam crabs for the fumet base:

8 cups water

1 tablespoon salt

6 live blue crabs (about 3 pounds total)

For the bisque base:

4 tablespoons butter

1 leek, trimmed to 1 inch above white base, halved
   horizontally, well rinsed, and finely chopped

1 onion, halved and finely chopped

2 ribs celery, finely chopped

Salt and freshly ground black pepper

1 teaspoon Old Bay Seasoning

4 tablespoons all-purpose flour

Reserved shells from the crab fumet

$3/4$ cup dry vermouth

Reserved fumet base

2 bay leaves

To finish the bisque:

2 tablespoons butter

1 large shallot, finely chopped (about $1/2$ cup)

Salt and freshly ground black pepper

$1/2$ teaspoon Old Bay Seasoning

3 tablespoons all-purpose flour

Reserved bisque base

1 cup heavy cream

8 ounces (1 cup) lump crabmeat

Reserved meat from steamed blue crabs (about
   $1/4$ cup)

1 tablespoon finely chopped fresh thyme leaves

To make the fumet base, bring the water and salt to a vigorous boil in a $5^{1}/_{2}$-quart Dutch oven or similarly sized pot. Add the crabs all at once (see Cooking Crustaceans, page 90). Cover and reduce to a high simmer over medium-high heat. Cook for 8 minutes. Remove crabs from the pot and set aside to cool. Strain the cooking liquid through a very fine sieve or chinois lined with 2 or 3 paper towels into a large bowl. Set aside.

continued >

COOKING CRUSTACEANS

As you read in the opening to this chapter, crushed crustacean shells are a crucial part of building the flavor in most bisque soups. Shells from a previously cooked lobster or crab don't emit the same level of flavor as uncooked shells. This is because that intense shell flavor seeps into the fumet base as they are cooking, and that's where most of it stays. Since their internal organs and flesh rot very quickly when dead, both crabs and lobster really must be put into the pot alive.

Submerging live creatures into boiling water may seem very cruel, but there are ways to minimize the pain, for both the crustacean and the cook. I place them in the freezer for about 30 minutes prior to cooking. This puts them into a sleepy, relaxed state and works for both crabs and lobsters. Get the water to a rolling boil, submerge all at once (headfirst for lobsters), cover, reduce to a low boil, and cook according to recipe directions.

When the crabs are cool, pull off their legs and set to the side of your work surface. Pull off their backs, rinse well, and add to the shell pile. Pull the little tab up on the bottom of their bodies to release the bottom of the crab and expose the interior meat, remove the tab and the bottom of the crab shell, and add to the shell pile. Remove and discard the gills, which look like white, feathery matter, and rinse off any bitter green matter, also called "tomalley." Carefully work inside the bodies to remove any sweet flesh, and be attentive to removing and discarding any bits of shell or cartilage. Reserve the meat in the fridge. With a mallet or the bottom of a sturdy saucepan, smash the reserved shells into smaller bits. This will help them to release flavor in the next step of the bisque journey, and probably the most important one—the bisque base.

To prepare the bisque base, rinse the crab-cooking pot and use it to melt the butter over medium heat. Add the leek, onion, celery, a generous dash of salt and pepper, and Old Bay Seasoning. Stir to coat, cooking 5 minutes, or until just softened. Add the flour, stir, and cook for 1 minute. Add the reserved shells, stir to coat, and cook for 2 minutes. Add the vermouth, increase heat to high, and cook down to a glaze. Add the reserved strained fumet base, 2 bay leaves, and a generous pinch of salt. Bring to a boil over high heat, then reduce to a simmer over medium/medium-low heat. Cook uncovered for 25 minutes, skimming off foam and discarding as you go. Strain through a China cap or fine colander into a large bowl, pressing hard against the solids to release flavor before discarding them. Set the bisque base aside.

To finish the bisque, rinse the same cooking pot again and melt the butter over medium heat. Add the shallot, a dash of salt and pepper, and Old Bay Seasoning. Stir to coat, and cook until just softened, about 5 minutes. Add the flour, stir to coat, and cook for 1 minute. Add the reserved bisque base. Bring to a high simmer over high heat. Reduce to a low simmer over medium-low heat. Cook, uncovered for 10 minutes. Stir in the cream, lump crabmeat, and reserved blue crabmeat. Cook over medium heat for 5 minutes just to heat through. Taste carefully and adjust seasoning with salt and pepper. Stir gently to avoid breaking up the lump crab, stirring in the thyme at the last minute.

BISQUE DE HOMARD
Lobster Bisque

(MAKES 8 TO 10 SERVINGS)

This creamy, delicate soup is infused from start to finish with the luxurious flavor of lobster. The method is exactly the same as the crab bisque and also can be done in three stages: fumet base, bisque base, and finishing. The first two can be done ahead and refrigerated or frozen, but finishing with the cream and fresh herbs needs to be done just before serving. If you absolutely cannot find live lobster for this recipe, substitute 6 (^{1}/$_2$-pound) uncooked lobster tails. Like many traditional bisques, this one uses rice as the thickening agent. The result is frothier than using a roux. The sweetness of cognac and the lively licorice flavor of tarragon make a beautiful finish to this classic bisque favorite.

To steam the lobster for the fumet base:

12 cups water

1 teaspoon sea salt or kosher salt

2 (1^3/$_4$-pound) live lobsters

For the bisque base:

4 tablespoons unsalted butter

1 leek, trimmed to 1 inch above the white root, halved vertically, well rinsed and coarsely chopped

1 onion, coarsely chopped

2 ribs celery, coarsely chopped

2 medium Roma tomatoes, coarsely chopped

Salt and freshly ground black pepper

Reserved crushed shells from the fumet base

Reserved strained fumet base

5 sprigs fresh thyme

2 bay leaves

To finish the bisque:

4 tablespoons unsalted butter

1 leek, trimmed to 1 inch above the white root, halved vertically, well rinsed, and coarsely chopped

1 large shallot, coarsely chopped (about ^{1}/$_2$ cup)

Salt and freshly ground black pepper

^{1}/$_4$ cup Arborio or basmati rice

1 cup plus 1 tablespoon good-quality cognac, divided

Reserved strained bisque base

Reserved chopped lobster meat, divided

1 cup heavy cream

1 tablespoon finely chopped fresh chives

1 tablespoon finely chopped fresh tarragon leaves

For the fumet base, bring the water and salt to a furious boil, covered, over high heat. Meanwhile, chill and calm the lobsters (see Cooking Crustaceans, page 90). Submerge each lobster headfirst into the boiling water, reduce to a high simmer over medium-high heat, and cook for 8 minutes. They will be bright red all over when cooked. Remove lobsters and submerge in

continued >

ice water for 2 minutes to shock and stop the cooking. Set aside. Strain the fumet (lobster cooking water) through a fine colander or chinois lined with 2 or 3 paper towels into a large bowl. Set aside. Rinse the cooking pot and set it aside.

Break down the cooked lobster. Assemble two piles on your work surface as you go along—one of the shells and one of the meat. A lobster has three parts containing meat: the legs, the claws/claw joints, and the tail. For the purposes of this bisque, the leg meat (a very small amount) is left in the legs, which are pounded and thus give their flavor to the bisque base. The tail and claw meat is extracted and reserved for the finished bisque. Here is how to do it: With your non-dominant hand, grasp the body and firmly twist the legs off of the first lobster. Place the legs in the "shell" pile on your work surface. Next, tear off the two claws by holding firmly and twisting to release from the body. Pull off the tail from the body, and then rinse off any green tomalley from the base of the tail. Discard the head and body.

To extract the meat from each claw and two front joints, pound the entire length of the claw with a mallet or small saucepan. Pull the claw from the front joints, pounding a bit further if needed. Pull the smaller, lower part of the claw down from the big, meaty part of the claw and this should start to release the claw meat. Pound both parts of the claw with a mallet if needed to extract the rest of the meat. Then do the same to release the meat from the front claw joints. Repeat with the second claw. Add the shells to the shell pile, and then wipe down your work surface (there will be some liquid). Chop the meat into coarse, $1/2$-inch chunks and reserve in the "meat" pile. To extract the meat from the tail, cut through the cartilage along the bottom side of the tail with kitchen scissors. Spread the cartilage slightly to reveal the tail meat, and gently pry it loose. Add the tail shell to the shell pile, and then cut the tail meat into $1/2$-inch chunks and reserve in the meat pile. Repeat with the second lobster. With a large chef's knife, coarsely cut the shells in the shell pile into large pieces to maximize flavor release. You will have about 2 cups meat and a big pile of shells. Reserve both separately.

To prepare the bisque base, rinse the cooking pot and melt the butter in it over medium heat. Add the leek, onion, celery, tomatoes, and salt and pepper. Stir to coat. Cook uncovered for 10 minutes, or until softened and the tomatoes start to break down. Add the reserved shells, strained fumet, thyme, bay leaves, and a generous pinch of salt. Bring to a boil over high heat, reduce to a simmer over medium/medium-low heat, and cook uncovered for 40 minutes, skimming off and discarding any foam along the way. Strain through a China cap or fine colander into a large bowl, pressing hard against the solids with a ladle to extract flavor. Reserve the strained bisque base and discard solids. Rinse or wash the cooking pot.

To finish the bisque, melt the butter over medium heat in the Dutch oven or cooking pot. Add leek, shallot, and salt and pepper. Stir to coat and cook for 5 minutes, or until vegetables are just softened. Stir in the rice, and "toast" it to a very pale golden brown, about 2 minutes. Increase heat to high, then add 1 cup cognac and cook down to a glaze, about 30 seconds. Add the strained bisque base, bring to a boil over high, and reduce to a medium simmer over medium/medium-low heat. Season lightly with salt and pepper. Cook uncovered for 30 minutes, or until the rice is very soft. Remove from the heat. Add half of the reserved lobster meat (about 1 cup). Using a blender, or food processor, process until the base is frothy smooth, dividing into batches if needed. (*Note:* Stop here if storing overnight in the refrigerator.)

To finish, in the same pot, bring the base to a low boil over medium-high heat. Stir in the cream, remaining 1 tablespoon cognac, and remaining lobster meat. Cook until very hot, about 3 minutes. Taste carefully and adjust seasoning as needed. Serve in individual bowls or a tureen, garnished with a flurry of fresh herbs over the top.

Variation: This bisque would be delicious with an additional warm garnish of finely sliced leeks, sautéed until soft in butter and seasoned.

BISQUE DE CREVETTES
Shrimp Bisque

(MAKES 8 SERVINGS)

It never ceases to amaze me how tiny, fragile, so-thin-they're-transparent shrimp shells come packed with such potent flavor. As I was making the fumet for this bisque, fresh, sweet scents of the sea wafted my way. Although it can be prepped in two stages, this magnificent bisque comes together in minutes. And, mercifully, because they are significantly less prone to spoilage and bacteria than lobster and crabs, shrimp do not require being cooked alive. The most work and time will involve removing the shells and deveining the shrimp. Then you are ready to roll. The elegance of this soup belies its ease of preparation, making it an appropriate and seductive start for a special-occasion meal.

1 pound medium-size (16-20 count) shell-on raw
shrimp

For the bisque base:

4 tablespoons unsalted butter

1 medium onion, coarsely chopped

2 ribs celery, coarsely chopped

1 leek, trimmed to 1 inch above the white root,
halved vertically, well-rinsed, and coarsely
chopped

2 cloves garlic, smashed and chopped

Salt and freshly ground black pepper

Reserved shrimp shells, coarsely chopped

2 small Roma tomatoes, coarsely chopped (skin on
and seeds in)

2 bay leaves

5 sprigs fresh thyme

$^2/_3$ cup good-quality Chardonnay

7 cups water

For the bisque:

4 tablespoons unsalted butter

1 large shallot, finely chopped (about $^1/_2$ cup)

2 small ribs celery, finely chopped

Salt and freshly ground black pepper

5 tablespoons all-purpose flour

$^1/_2$ cup dry vermouth

Reserved bisque base

Half of the reserved fresh shrimp (about 1 cup),
chopped into $^1/_4$-inch dice

To finish the bisque:

Remaining reserved shrimp (about 1 cup), chopped
into $^1/_4$-inch dice

2 tablespoons finely chopped chives

$^1/_2$ cup whole cream

Salt and freshly ground black pepper

Finely diced tomato (optional)

Finely chopped fresh chives (optional)

To ready the shrimp, cut through the shells and the top of the vein on the arched, outer edge of the shrimp's back. Cut all the way down to the tail, then spread the shell around the opening and peel

continued >

it off. Using your fingertips, or a paring knife if necessary, scrape out the vein (there is not always one there) and discard. Carefully rinse the shrimp and the shells, and reserve each separately on your work surface.

To prepare the bisque base, melt the butter in a 5 1/2-quart Dutch oven or similarly sized pot over medium heat. Add the onion, celery, leek, garlic, and salt and pepper. Stir to coat, and cook for 5 minutes, until just softened. Add the reserved chopped shrimp shells and tomatoes. Stir to coat, and cook for 1 minute. Add bay leaves, thyme, and Chardonnay. Increase heat to high and cook uncovered until the wine has cooked down to a glaze. Add water and season lightly with salt and pepper; bring to a boil over high heat. Reduce to medium, then cook uncovered for 25 minutes, skimming off and discarding any foam on top. Strain the stock through a China cap or fine colander into a large bowl, pressing hard to extract the flavor from the solids. Discard the solids.

Rinse or wash the cooking pot and prepare the bisque. Melt the butter over medium heat. Add shallot and celery, and season lightly with salt and pepper. Stir to coat. Cook 5 minutes, or until just softened. Scatter the flour evenly over the sautéed vegetables, stir to coat, and cook 1 minute. Whisk in the vermouth and cook for 1 minute. Add the reserved strained bisque base, bring to a boil, uncovered, over high heat, reduce to a simmer, and cook for 15 minutes. Add half of the reserved shrimp, stir, and cook for 1 minute, until just opaque. Using a blender or food processor, purée the bisque until smooth (about 2 minutes).

To finish, return the bisque to the pot and bring to a simmer over medium heat. Cook uncovered until reduced by about 1/2 cup, 10 to 15 minutes. (*Note:* You can stop here and refrigerate the bisque overnight.) Just before serving, heat the bisque over medium heat and add the reserved shrimp, chives, and cream. Taste carefully and adjust seasoning as needed. Serve very hot and garnish with a smattering of finely diced tomato and fresh chives if desired.

BISQUE DE PALOURDES AUX CONFETTIS DE LÉGUMES
Clam Bisque with Vegetable Confetti
(MAKES 8 SERVINGS)

Tender cherrystone clams give beautiful brine flavor to the fumet base, which is later speckled with a colorful array of tiny diced vegetables in this magnificent bisque. It is important to take the time to rinse the clams well, picking out and discarding any that look cracked or broken. Soaking the clams in milk for an hour will draw out any internal grit that might muddy the bisque, so don't miss this step. If you can't find cherrystone clams, substitute Pacific littleneck or another tender, short-necked clam.

3 pounds cherrystone clams (about 48)

4 cups milk

For the fumet base:

Rinsed, prepped clams

2 cups Chardonnay

2 cups water

1 teaspoon salt

5 sprigs fresh thyme, bundled with kitchen string

For the bisque:

5 pieces bacon, cut into ⅛-inch thick strips

3 ribs celery, finely chopped

2 leeks, trimmed to 1 inch above the white root, halved vertically, well rinsed, and finely chopped

1 medium onion, finely chopped

2 carrots, peeled, quartered vertically, and finely chopped

Salt and freshly ground black pepper

4 San Marzano canned whole tomatoes, finely chopped (or substitute fresh plum tomatoes)

4 tablespoons unsalted butter

4 tablespoons all-purpose flour

⅔ cup good-quality Chardonnay

4 cups reserved strained fumet base

1½ cups heavy cream

2 tablespoons finely chopped fresh parsley

2 tablespoons finely chopped fresh chives

Reserved clams

In a large bowl, cover the clams with fresh water. Using your hands, slosh the clams about to loosen any external grit. Repeat, changing the water 2 or 3 times, until the water in the bowl is clear. Discard any broken or damaged-looking clams. Place the clams in a fresh bowl and cover with milk. Toss lightly and allow to rest in the milk for 30 minutes to 1 hour. Strain the milk (discarding) through a colander, then rinse the clams again, very thoroughly. Set aside.

To prepare the fumet base, place the cleaned clams in an 8-quart Dutch oven or similarly sized pot. Add the Chardonnay, water, salt, and thyme bundle. Bring to a boil over high heat,

continued >

covered, and cook until the clams have just opened, about 5 minutes. Remove the clams using a slotted spoon and place into a bowl to cool. Line a China cap or fine colander with two paper towels. Carefully strain the steaming liquid into a bowl and reserve. When the clams are cool enough to handle, gently pull out the clam from each open shell, and discard the shells. Reserve the clams in a small bowl.

To finish the bisque, place the bacon in a 5 1/2-quart Dutch oven or similarly sized pot over medium-high heat. Cook the bacon, stirring every few minutes, until thoroughly browned and all of the fat is rendered. Remove with a slotted spoon and reserve on a paper towel to drain. Reduce heat to medium. Add the celery, leeks, onion, carrots, and salt and pepper to taste. Cook over medium heat for 15 minutes, stirring, until softened and cooked through (do not brown!).

Add the tomatoes and butter. Stir to combine. When the butter is melted, stir in the flour and cook for 1 minute. Add the Chardonnay, increase heat to high, and cook down to a glaze, about 1 minute. Add the reserved fumet, bring to a boil over high heat, uncovered, and reduce to a simmer. Cook for 5 minutes. Add the cream and cook together another 5 minutes. At the very last minute, add the parsley, chives, and reserved clams and any of their juices. Taste, and adjust seasonings as needed. The bacon can either be stirred into the bisque at this point, or used as a garnish for each bowl. Serve very hot.

Bisque d'Huitres et de Panais
Oyster and Parsnip Bisque

(MAKES 8 TO 10 SERVINGS)

Parsnips and oysters may sound like odd bisque-fellows, but they actually make a lot of sense. Panais, *like turnips, are sweet, lovely root vegetables frequently used in French kitchens. Their sweetness plays beautifully with the oysters, and the starch in the parsnips gives a velvety texture to this heavenly bisque. Even better, since oyster shells don't yield much in terms of flavor, there is no fumet base preparation involved for this bisque. Rather, the oyster flavor comes from the brine they're stored in, as well as the oysters themselves, which are stirred in at the very end. If making this soup ahead, hold off and add the oysters and cream just before serving. Willapoint oysters, readily available in their brine in the refrigerator section of most fish counters at the grocery, are firm and meaty. Use the freshest raw oysters you can find, and don't discard the brine except into the soup pot. It is one of the flavor keys to the bisque.*

6 tablespoons unsalted butter

1 leek, trimmed to 1 inch above the white root, halved vertically, well rinsed and finely chopped

2 medium shallots, finely chopped (about 1 cup)

2 medium parsnips, peeled, quartered vertically, and finely chopped

1 tablespoon finely chopped fresh thyme leaves

Salt and freshly ground black pepper

1/2 cup dry vermouth, plus 1 tablespoon optional

1/2 cup good-quality Chardonnay

4 tablespoons all-purpose flour

4 cups good-quality, low sodium boxed seafood/fish stock or homemade Fish Stock (see page 17)

1 cup finely chopped oyster or chanterelle mushrooms, tough feet removed

3 (8-ounce packages) Willapoint Oysters (3 cups)

1 cup heavy cream

1 tablespoon finely chopped fresh thyme leaves

In a 5 1/2-quart Dutch oven or similarly sized pot, melt the butter over medium heat. Add the leek, shallots, parsnips, and thyme and season with salt and pepper. Stir to coat. Cook over medium heat, stirring several times, for 15 minutes, until all the vegetables have softened (do not let them color). Add the 1/2 cup vermouth, increase heat to medium-high, and cook down to a glaze, 1 to 2 minutes. Add the Chardonnay and cook down to a glaze, 1 to 2 minutes. Scatter the flour evenly over the pot and stir to combine. Whisk in the fish stock, and bring to a boil over high heat. Reduce to medium/medium-low and cook uncovered for 15 minutes, skimming off any initial foam/scum that rises to the top.

Purée until frothy smooth with a blender or food processor. Return to the pot, if necessary. Add the mushrooms, oysters, and cream. Bring to a simmer over medium-high heat, reduce to medium, and cook through for 5 to 8 minutes, until the oysters are firm and opaque. Taste, and adjust seasonings as needed. Finish with 1 tablespoon of vermouth, if desired, and fresh thyme. Serve very hot.

CHAPTER 7

LES DAUBES
Classic Stews

Daube is the French word for stew, especially when using tough, inexpensive cuts of meat (such as shoulder or chuck) that is braised in wine with vegetable aromatics. Sometimes, as with Bœuf à la Bourguignonne (page 107), Coq au Vin (page 109), or Daube à la Provençale (page 118) the meats are marinated in wine overnight before braising. Classic *daube* preparations were typically peasant fare and infused with various flavorings, including cinnamon, cloves, prunes, olives, and more.

Every recipe in this chapter was prepared in one of my Le Creuset ceramic-coated cast-iron Dutch ovens—some of my best friends in the kitchen. If you don't own one, use the best-quality heavy-bottom stockpot or stew pot at your disposal. Dutch ovens are oven safe, but I prefer to simmer my daubes on the stovetop because it is easier to skim, taste, and generally keep an eye on what's happening there, without opening and closing the oven door and manipulating a heavy pot. If you prefer an oven to the stovetop, please follow these recipes as they are, but do the cooking in a moderate 325-degree-F oven for the same amount of time as specified for the stovetop.

Poulet Pinot Gris avec Champignons, Poireaux, et Moutarde Dijon

Chicken Braised in Pinot Gris with Mushrooms, Leeks, and Dijon Mustard

(MAKES 4 TO 6 SERVINGS)

Braising chicken in wine is the basic formula for a dish called coq au vin. *Braising meat in wine is at the heart of the cooking action for most of the recipes in this chapter. The kind of wine used, though typically a red (especially a Burgundy), can really be any grape varietal, including Alsace-inspired Pinot Gris for this especially delicious and slightly sweet version. Interpretations of this stunning French stew can be found throughout France, but the classic garnishes typically include* lardons *(or substitute bacon), mushrooms, and onions. This stew really should be made a day ahead to enrich the flavors. If you choose to do so, add the cream and mustard just before serving. It is exquisite alongside a mound of tender, buttered spaghetti.*

3-4 large bone-in chicken breasts (about 3¹/₂ pounds), cut horizontally into 4 equal pieces

Salt and freshly ground black pepper

1 tablespoon unsalted butter

1 tablespoon olive oil

1 medium onion, halved and thinly sliced

3 cloves garlic, smashed and finely chopped

1 leek, white and palest green part only, halved vertically, cleaned (see The Nitty-Gritty on Leeks, page 45), and thinly sliced

8 ounces (about 2 cups) white button mushrooms, stems trimmed, cleaned (see How to Clean Mushrooms, page 47), and sliced about ¹/₄ inch thick

2 tablespoons all-purpose flour

3 cups good-quality Pinot Gris or Riesling

1 tablespoon finely chopped fresh thyme leaves

¹/₃ cup heavy cream*

2 tablespoons finely chopped fresh parsley

1 tablespoon Dijon mustard

Hot buttered noodles or pasta for serving

Fresh thyme sprigs, for garnish (optional)

Prep the chicken, removing excess fat, skin, and any stray, spindly rib or spine bones. Season generously with salt and pepper on all sides.

Heat the butter and olive oil in a 5¹/₂-quart Dutch oven over high heat. When it is bubbling, add the chicken in a single layer, skin side down. Reduce heat to medium-high and cook for 3 minutes, or until the skin is golden brown. Turn all of the chicken pieces and cook another 3 minutes on the second side. Using tongs, remove the chicken from the pan and reserve (the inversed

Dutch oven lid makes a good "plate" for this purpose).

Reduce heat to medium-low. Add the onion, garlic, leek, and a dusting of salt and pepper. Stir to coat. Cook, stirring, for 5 minutes, or until the vegetables have softened but not browned. Add the mushrooms, stir to combine, and cook another 3 minutes. Dust the flour evenly over the top, stir to combine, and cook 1 minute.

Increase the heat to high and add the wine, stirring vigorously with a wooden spoon to pick up any brown bits. Bring to a boil, then reduce to a simmer. Stir in the thyme. Return the reserved chicken to the pot, arranging in a single layer; about three-fourths of the chicken should be covered with the wine. Cook uncovered for 35 minutes, or until the chicken is completely cooked and free of any pink juices. Test for doneness by inserting a paring knife into the thickest part of a chicken breast. When cooked, remove the chicken and reserve.

Increase the heat to high and reduce the cooking liquid by about a third; this takes about 3 minutes. Taste, and adjust seasonings as needed. (*Note*: If serving the following day, return the chicken to the pan, cool, and refrigerate overnight.) To finish the stew just before serving, whisk in the cream, parsley, and mustard and heat through. Serve warm over buttered egg noodles or a broad pasta such as pappardelle. Garnish with fresh thyme sprigs.

Do not substitute half & half or milk.

BŒUF À LA BOURGUIGNONNE
Burgundy Beef Stew

(MAKES 6 TO 8 SERVINGS)

This remarkably delicious daube hails from Burgundy, as the name implies. Its three-tiered, time-tested cooking process renders the humblest cuts of meat and vegetable aromatics into one of France's most revered dishes, and one of my personal favorites. This dish produces celestial, savory aromas as it simmers its way into deliciousness over the course of several, mostly untended, hours. Marinated overnight, the beef assumes the rich color of the red wine and flavors of the vegetables and herbs that surround it. After, the beef is seared in bacon fat, thickened with a bit of flour, and cooked further with the vegetables and wine. The final step is straining the whole pot, discarding the vegetables and herb bundle, and returning the beef to the wine sauce. It is finished with mushrooms and pearl onions, each sautéed separately and returned to the pot just before serving. It may look like a lot of work, but it really boils down to the three steps outlined above (marinate, cook, and strain/finish), which can all be done ahead.

I use rib-eye steaks in this recipe because I like the flavor and texture of the cut. Feel free to substitute a more typical "stew" cut, such as short ribs, chuck, or round. But if you do so, you will need to cook the stew considerably longer, at least 2 to 3 hours total, until the tougher cuts have broken down into fork-yielding tenderness. The wine used for the marinade does not necessarily need to be a Burgundy, but choose a good-quality red with a nice roundness and very delicate touch of sweet. I like Cabernet Sauvignon. Serve over broad egg noodles, soft polenta, or with mashed potatoes.

For the marinade:

2 pounds rib-eye steak, excess fat trimmed away,
  cut into 2-inch cubes

1 onion, cut into 8 coarse chunks

2 ribs celery, cut into 2-inch lengths

2 carrots, peeled and cut into 2-inch lengths

8 sprigs each fresh thyme and parsley, bundled
  with kitchen string

2 bay leaves

5 black peppercorns

3 cups good-quality Cabernet Sauvignon, Pinot Noir,
  or Burgundy

For the stew:

Reserved marinated beef

Salt and freshly ground black pepper

4 slices bacon, cut into 1/4-inch dice

Reserved marinated aromatic vegetables

1 tablespoon tomato paste

2 tablespoons all-purpose flour

Reserved wine from marinade

1/2 cup beef stock

For the onions:

10 ounces (about 2 cups) pearl onions

2 tablespoons unsalted butter

Salt and freshly ground black pepper

1 teaspoon finely chopped fresh thyme

1 tablespoon extra dry vermouth

1/2 cup beef stock

For the mushrooms:

2 tablespoons unsalted butter

2 cups coarsely chopped shiitake mushrooms,
  tough feet trimmed

Salt and freshly ground black pepper

Fresh parsley, for garnish

continued >

Up to 24 hours before cooking, assemble the marinade. In a 5½-quart Dutch oven or large bowl, combine the beef, onion, celery, carrots, herb bundle, bay leaves, peppercorns, and wine. Stir to combine thoroughly, pressing the beef and vegetables down into the wine. Cover and refrigerate overnight, or for a minimum of 6 hours, stirring two or three times along the way to ensure equal distribution of the marinade.

To prepare the stew, remove the beef cubes from the marinade with a fork and dry well on paper towels. Season generously on all sides with salt and pepper.

Place the bacon in a 5½-quart Dutch oven, breaking up with your fingers to distribute. Cook over medium-high, stirring occasionally, until lightly browned and the fat is mostly rendered. Remove bacon from the pot with a slotted spoon and drain on paper towels. Reserve.

Brown the beef in a single layer in the rendered bacon fat over medium-high heat, about 3 minutes per side. (Do not crowd the beef in the pot. It's better to cook in batches for maximum browning and flavor.) Remove with a slotted spoon and reserve on a plate or on the inversed Dutch oven lid. Repeat as needed. Reserve.

Using a China cap or fine colander, strain the vegetables from the wine marinade, plucking out the herb bundle and setting it aside temporarily. Reserve the wine from the marinade in a separate bowl. Sauté the vegetables in the Dutch oven until softened, stirring once or twice, about 5 minutes. Add the tomato paste, stir to combine, and cook through for 1 minute. Drizzle the flour evenly over the top of the vegetables, stir to coat, and cook through another minute.

Return the reserved wine marinade and beef stock to the pot, stirring with a wooden spoon to pick up any browned bits. Bring to a boil over high heat, and then reduce to a simmer over low heat. Return the reserved bacon, beef, and herb bundle to the pot. Season lightly with salt and pepper. Cover and cook at a very low simmer for 45 minutes, stirring occasionally. (*Note*: If you have substituted a tougher cut such as ribs, round, or chuck, you will need to cook the stew base longer, about 2 to 3 hours, or until the beef is very tender. The cooking can also be done in a low oven, about 325 degrees F, instead of on the stovetop.)

To finish the stew, strain all the solids through a China cap, reserving the cooking liquid and the beef and discarding the herb bundle and vegetables. Return the beef to the pot and keep warm at a simmer. Taste, and adjust seasonings as needed. If you like, you can stop here, cool off the stew, and refrigerate it overnight before finishing with the onion and mushroom garnishes.

To prepare the onions for peeling, submerge them in water in a small bowl. Either heat in the microwave on high for 1 minute, or cover with boiling water and let sit for 1 to 2 minutes. The pesky peels will come right off with a paring knife. Heat the butter in a medium sauté pan over medium heat. Add the onions, salt and pepper to taste, and thyme; toss to coat. Cook until just starting to color, about 5 minutes. Add the vermouth and cook down to a glaze. Add the beef stock and cook on a low simmer until tender all the way through, about 12 minutes. Increase heat to high to cook off any remaining liquid. Taste, and adjust seasonings as needed. Reserve warm.

For the mushrooms, heat the butter in large sauté pan over medium heat. Add the mushrooms and season lightly with salt and pepper. Toss to coat. Cook about 5 minutes, or until the mushrooms have softened. Reserve warm.

To serve, reheat the stew thoroughly over medium heat. Ladle into individual bowls. Top each with several onions and a smattering of mushrooms. Garnish with fresh parsley if desired. Alternatively, present it in a tureen.

COQ AU VIN
Chicken Braised in Red Wine
(MAKES 6 TO 8 SERVINGS)

The process for making a traditional coq au vin *such as this is almost exactly the same as preparing a Bœuf à la Bourguignonne. The only differences are that the beef is exchanged for chicken, beef stock is exchanged for chicken stock, and the whole dish is cooked slightly longer. This recipe, then, is really a variation on the theme of Bœuf à la Bourguignonne and is presented as such in the directions that follow. Like its beef stew cousin,* coq au vin *is traditionally served with the mushroom and onion garnishes. However, because it also pairs so magically with glazed turnips, there is a recipe for those* délices *provided (see page 111). Why not use all three? They are lovely together— earthy, slightly sweet, and sublime—and so utterly French.*

COQ AU VIN VARIATIONS:

Use the same recipe as Bœuf à la Bourguignonne (see page 107), except change out the beef quantity for 1 (5-pound) chicken cut into 9 pieces, substitute the ½ cup beef stock under "For the stew" with 1 cup of chicken stock, and braise for 1 hour and 15 minutes in a larger, 8-quart Dutch oven if possible. All the rest remains the same. As always, season carefully.

TURNED VEGETABLES

I first learned about "turning" vegetables at Le Cordon Bleu, but it really didn't become a habit until I spent many long afternoons practicing the technique, after the morning's cooking work was done, at Fauchon gourmet food shop and affiliated restaurant. The other rookies and I would turn vegetables for hours, staring out at the gray Parisian skies and filling huge bins with prettily shaped potatoes, turnips, carrots, zucchini, parsnips, and more. There are two benefits to using turned vegetables: The similar sizes ensures even cooking time, and the presentation is pretty.

For many of the stews in this chapter, the garnish vegetables are typically turned or shaped into approximately 2-inch-long, 1 inch-thick ovals, kind of like mini footballs. No matter what kind of vegetable you're starting with, the first step is to cut them into rectangular lengths of the approximate dimensions above. Then, holding the individual length

in your non-dominant hand, slowly turn the vegetable, cutting down with a paring knife to remove the sharp edges, and round the vegetable into an attractive oval. A turning or peeling knife with a sharp, curved cutting edge (like a scythe), is the best to use for turning, but a sharp paring knife works almost as well.

Navets Glacé
Sugar-and-Butter-Glazed Turnips
(MAKES 6 SERVINGS)

The French love their turnips, and this simple preparation makes them especially love-worthy. The nuttiness of sautéed butter paired with just a sprinkle of sugar and some fresh parsley at the finish make them just about perfect fresh out of the sauté pan, but they are really lovely combined with the homespun, elegant French goodness of a Coq au Vin. Add these to your repertoire as a side for a simple roast chicken, or just about anything, when they are in peak season in the cooler months of fall and spring. Look for firm-skinned turnips with a purple blush and a heavy weight for their size.

5 medium turnips, peeled

2 tablespoons unsalted butter

Salt and freshly ground black pepper

$3/4$ cup Chicken Stock (see page 18)

1 teaspoon granulated sugar

1 tablespoon finely chopped fresh parsley

To prepare the turnips, cut through the $1/4$-inch-thick second skin by bearing down with a paring knife as you work your way around the turnip. Halve the peeled turnips and cut into $1/2$-inch-thick slices. You will end up with about 4 cups.

Melt the butter in a large sauté pan over medium heat. Add the turnips and season generously with salt and pepper. Toss to coat, cooking for about 2 minutes to soften. Add the chicken stock and sugar. Cover with a square of parchment paper cut approximately to meet the size of the pan (this will help keep the steam close to the turnips and cook them without drying them out). Bring to a boil over high heat, and then reduce to a simmer, stirring once or twice. Cook for 10 minutes, or until soft in the center when pierced with a knife. Remove the parchment and discard. Increase the heat to medium-high and continue cooking until the liquid has cooked off and the turnips are lightly colored and shimmering from the sugar. Taste, and adjust seasonings as needed. Serve warm, garnished with fresh parsley.

Note: The turnips can be made a day ahead and reheated gently before serving.

Navarin d'Agneau
Lamb and Vegetable Stew

(MAKES 6 TO 8 SERVINGS)

This beloved French stew bundles many of the superstars of spring—lamb, onions, potatoes—and turnips into a single pot and one super stew. A long, slow braising of lamb shoulder with vegetable aromatics starts the flavor build-up, and the dish is later finished with another fresh batch of onions, potatoes, and turnips, with blanched fresh green beans added at the very end to preserve their bright flavor. This recipe uses lamb shoulder because it frequently comes with bones (later removed), which give a huge flavor boost during the braising process, but feel free to substitute leg of lamb or another tough cut suitable for braising. A splash of fresh orange juice, fennel seeds, and a bundle of thyme lend a spring-like brightness to this stunning stew. Remember to skim the fat off the top of the stew as it braises, using a ladle and a nearby bowl of water to dispose of the fat deposits.

3 pounds lamb shoulder, trimmed and cut into 2- to 3-inch cubes (reserve any bones)

Salt and freshly ground black pepper

2 tablespoons unsalted butter

2 tablespoons olive oil

1 onion, quartered

1 carrot, peeled and cut into 2-inch lengths

2 ribs celery, cut into 2-inch lengths

1 leek, trimmed to 1 inch above the white base, halved vertically, cleaned (see The Nitty-Gritty on Leeks, page 45), and cut into 2-inch lengths

4 cloves garlic, smashed

1 tablespoon tomato paste

2 tablespoons all-purpose flour

4 cups water

2 bay leaves

1 teaspoon fennel seeds

1/2 teaspoon dried Valencia orange peel (or substitute 1 teaspoon fresh orange zest)

1/3 cup freshly squeezed orange juice

Tiny pinch of ground cloves

5 sprigs fresh thyme, bundled with kitchen string

For the finishing vegetable garnishes:

2 cups peeled pearl onions

1 cup small white new potatoes, skin on, well scrubbed

3 large turnips, peeled and cut into 2-inch chunks

2 cups fresh green beans cut into 1-inch pieces

2 tablespoons butter (optional)

1 1/2 tablespoons finely chopped fresh thyme

Salt and freshly ground black pepper

Season the lamb shoulder cubes on all sides with salt and pepper. In an 8-quart Dutch oven, melt together the butter and olive oil over medium-high heat. When sizzling, add the prepped lamb and any bones. Arrange in a single layer and cook in batches to avoid overcrowding the pan. Brown over high heat, 4 minutes on each side. Remove the meat with a slotted spoon and reserve meat on a plate or Dutch oven lid nearby.

Drain off all but 2 tablespoons of the fat. Add the onion, carrot, celery, and leek. Season lightly with salt and pepper. Sweat over medium-low heat, stirring once or twice, for 5 minutes. Add the garlic and tomato paste and stir to coat thoroughly. Cook for 1 minute. Add the flour, stir to coat, and cook for 1 minute.

Return the seared lamb and its juices, along with the browned bones, to the Dutch oven with the water. Add bay leaves, fennel seeds, orange peel, orange juice, cloves, thyme bundle, and a dash of salt and freshly ground black pepper. Bring to a simmer over high heat, then reduce to medium-low and simmer gently, uncovered, for 1 hour and 15 minutes, or until the meat is extremely tender. Skim off fat as it reaches the top throughout the cooking process.

Strain the liquids through a China cap or fine colander into a large bowl. When cool enough to handle, pick the meat out of the strainer and set aside, trimming off any gristle and discarding any bones. Discard the vegetable solids and return the meat to the Dutch oven with the reserved cooking liquid. Taste, and adjust seasonings.

For the vegetables garnishes, add the onions, potatoes, and turnips to the Dutch oven. Stir to submerge. Bring to a simmer over high, reduce to low, and cook uncovered for 50 minutes, or until all of the vegetables are tender.

Meanwhile, blanch the green beans by cooking in well-salted boiling water for 4 minutes. Drain immediately and submerge in ice water. Strain and reserve. Just before serving, stir into the stew, or sauté separately in a pan with 2 tablespoons butter and thyme; season with salt and pepper, and keep warm. Ladle the stew into soup bowls and garnish with the warm sautéed beans, or serve the stew with the beans already stirred in. The stew stores beautifully overnight in the refrigerator for a day or two, but it is best to keep the beans separate for color and flavor freshness.

POT AU FEU
Boiled Beef

(MAKES 6 SERVINGS)

Pot au Feu is a centuries-old peasant dish that has worked its way into the hearts of the modern-day French. This is one-pot cooking at its finest. Unlike most of the other recipes in this chapter, the meat (beef here) is not browned. Instead, it is simmered in water (not wine) with beef marrowbones, which affords a silky, gelatinous texture to the jus. This jus is served over the sliced beef with a generous side of braised vegetables. A glorious Dijon mustard and horseradish cream, as well as cornichons and a baguette, are served alongside. Although it takes a long time to cook (about 4 hours), this is a wonderfully simple and inexpensive dish to prepare. Cloves and cinnamon give it a warm, almost medieval exoticism and makes the house smell like Christmas.

1 whole onion

5 whole cloves

2 pounds chuck roast

2 large beef marrowbones (about 1 pound)

7 cups water

1 rib celery, cut into 3 or 4 coarse chunks

2 bay leaves

1 teaspoon black peppercorns

2 teaspoons salt

1 cinnamon stick

5 sprigs thyme, bundled with kitchen string

For the vegetable garnish:

3 leeks, trimmed to 1 inch above the white part, halved vertically, cleaned, and tied firmly together with kitchen string

12 slender carrots, peeled and tied firmly together with kitchen string

1 large turnip, peeled about ¼ inch deep, halved, and cut into 16 large chunks about 2 inches each

1-2 cups water

Salt and freshly ground black pepper

For the Mustard Horseradish Cream Sauce:

½ cup cold heavy cream

1 heaping teaspoon prepared horseradish

1 heaping teaspoon Dijon mustard

Salt and freshly ground black pepper

Peel the onion. Insert the cloves into the onion, distributing evenly. Reserve.

In a 5½-quart Dutch oven, place the roast, marrowbones, water (adding more to cover, if needed), cloved onion, celery, bay leaves, peppercorns, salt, cinnamon stick, and thyme bundle. Bring to a bubbling simmer over high heat, then reduce to medium-low for a very low simmer. Do not boil! Cook uncovered for 2 hours, skimming off rising foam and scum frequently along the way.

Remove the marrowbones and discard. Using a fork, remove the roast from the pan and reserve nearby. Strain the cooking liquid through a China cap or fine colander into a large bowl. Press down on the solids with a ladle to extract maximum flavor, then discard the solids.

Return the roast to the Dutch oven with the cooking liquid. Place the leek bundle, carrot bundle, and turnips around the beef in the pan. Add more water to cover, about 1 to 2 cups. Taste, and adjust seasonings as needed. Bring to an aggressive simmer over medium-high heat, then reduce to medium-low. Tuck the vegetables down around the beef. Simmer gently, uncovered, for 45 minutes to 1 hour, or until the vegetables are very tender.

Meanwhile, prepare the Mustard Horseradish Cream Sauce. Combine all of the ingredients in a chilled medium-size bowl. Whisk vigorously to combine and mount into a soft whipped cream. Taste, and adjust seasonings. Refrigerate until ready to serve.

To finish and serve the pot au feu, remove the beef from the pot. When cool enough to handle, slice into even pieces, about $1/4$ inch thick, and arrange it in the middle of a large serving platter. Remove the vegetables from the pot and drain; arrange artfully around the beef in their bundles (minus the string). Cover to keep warm.

Meanwhile, reduce the cooking liquid over high heat until there are just 2 cups left. Taste, and adjust seasonings. Strain the solids through a colander and drizzle about $1/2$ cup of the juice over the meat and vegetables. Place the rest in a gravy boat or pitcher. Present with the jus and a bowl full of Mustard Horseradish Cream Sauce. If desired, scatter a dozen cornichon pickles around the platter.

DAUBE DE VEAU ET POMME À LA SAUGE
Veal, Apple, and Sage Stew

(MAKES 6 SERVINGS)

From a culinary standpoint, the Normandy region of France is known for two things: apples from its myriad orchards (thus cider and Calvados, an apple brandy) and dairy (thus cream and cheese) from its celebrated cows. It is a large and exquisite region, decorated with a quilt of hedged emerald-green fields, usually damp from a recent rain, with cattle almost incessantly mooing at a low, pleasing hum. This stew combines the sweet tartness of fresh cider and Granny Smith apples with the milky mildness of veal. Sage provides an earthy counterpoint that is just right, especially when finished with a splash of cream. Because the cider is such a big part of the stew, fresh is what you need and the best you can find.

1 tablespoon unsalted butter

1 tablespoon olive oil

2 1/2 pounds veal shoulder cut into 2-inch cubes

Salt and freshly ground black pepper

1 medium onion, finely chopped

4 cloves garlic, smashed and chopped

2 ribs celery, finely chopped

1 tablespoon dry rubbed or ground sage

2 tablespoons all-purpose flour

1 1/2 cups best-quality fresh apple cider

2 Granny Smith apples, peeled, cored, and cut into 1-inch cubes

1 1/2 cups beef or veal stock

1/3 cup whole cream or crème fraîche

1 tablespoon finely chopped fresh sage, for garnish

Melt the butter and olive oil over medium-high heat in a 5 1/2-quart Dutch oven or similarly sized pot. Meanwhile, pat the veal dry and season generously on all sides with salt and pepper. When the oil is just sizzling, arrange about half the veal in a single layer in the bottom of the pan; do not overcrowd. Cook until lightly browned, about 3 minutes. Turn and repeat on the second side. Remove the meat from the pan and reserve nearby. Repeat with remaining veal.

Reduce heat to medium-low. Add the onion, garlic, celery, sage, and a light sprinkle of salt and pepper. Stir to coat and cook for 5 minutes, or until just starting to soften. Return the reserved veal and any juices to the pot. Sprinkle the flour over the meat and vegetables, stirring to coat, and cook for 1 minute. Deglaze by adding the cider, stirring up any brown bits on the bottom or side of the pot. Bring to a boil over high heat and allow the cider to cook off and reduce for about 5 minutes.

Reduce heat to medium-low and establish a very gentle simmer. Add the apples and stock. Cook uncovered, continuing at a gentle simmer, until the veal is very tender, about 1 1/2 hours. Taste, and adjust seasoning as needed. (*Note*: You can stop here, allow to cool, and refrigerate overnight.)

Add the cream or créme fraîche (no other substitutes here, or it will curdle) and fresh sage at the last minute. Heat through and serve. This is delicious over rice or broad noodles.

DAUBE À LA PROVENÇALE
Provençal Beef Stew

(MAKES 8 SERVINGS)

Daubières are ceramic pots that resemble pitchers. They are used frequently in Provençal kitchens to lock in the steam as a daube slowly braises, making it very tender along the way. A good Dutch oven works just as well. A long marinade (up to 36 hours) in red wine with orange peel, cinnamon, aromatic vegetables, and orange juice makes for a delectable stew base. The stew is finished with sweet prunes, salty olives, bacon, lavender, and parsley. It becomes even better if it can sit overnight after cooking to further marry the exotic flavors. It is especially delicious served over fluffy basmati rice.

For the marinade:

3 pounds boneless beef ribs, cut into 2-inch cubes

Zest of 1 large orange, cut with a vegetable peeler into broad strips

5 sprigs each thyme and parsley, bundled with kitchen string

1 cinnamon stick

1 teaspoon black peppercorns

2 ribs celery, cut into 2-inch lengths

3 medium carrots, peeled and cut into 2-inch lengths

1 medium onion, quartered

4 large cloves garlic, smashed

3 bay leaves

$1/2$ teaspoon ground cloves

$1/3$ cup freshly squeezed orange juice

5 cups good-quality Cabernet Sauvignon

To finish the stew:

5 strips bacon, cut into $1/8$-inch-thick strips

Salt and freshly ground black pepper

2 medium onions, halved and thinly sliced

2 ribs celery, halved vertically and thinly sliced

2 medium carrots, peeled, halved vertically, and thinly sliced

1 leek, trimmed to 1 inch above the white root, halved vertically, cleaned, and thinly sliced

5 large cloves garlic, finely chopped

2 tablespoons tomato paste

2 tablespoons all-purpose flour

$1/2$ cup freshly squeezed orange juice

2 bay leaves

$1/2$ cup coarsely chopped pitted prunes

1 cup pitted kalamata olives

5 sprigs each fresh rosemary and fresh thyme, bundled with kitchen string

1 teaspoon dried lavender seeds

$1/4$ cup cognac or bourbon

For garnish:

$1/3$ cup finely chopped fresh parsley

Fine strips of zest from 1 orange

Warm cooked basmati rice (optional)

Up to 36 hours prior to cooking (and no less than 12 hours prior), combine all of the marinade ingredients together in an 8-quart Dutch oven or similarly sized sturdy cooking vessel. Cover and refrigerate until ready to cook, stirring every few hours. Remove beef with a fork and dry thoroughly with paper towels. Strain the marinade through a China cap into a large bowl, pressing down on the solids to extract the juice. Discard the solids and reserve the liquid.

To finish the stew, place the bacon strips in the Dutch oven over medium-high heat, and cook, stirring once or twice, until the fat is rendered and the bacon is browned, about 5 minutes. Remove bacon from pan with a slotted spoon and reserve.

Season the marinated beef with salt and pepper on all sides. (*Note*: Be careful with salt throughout this recipe, as the bacon and olives added near the end will increase the saltiness.) Drain off all but 2 tablespoons of the bacon fat. Arrange beef in a single layer in the Dutch oven; avoid crowding, and plan on at least two batches. Brown over medium-high heat for 3 minutes, turn, and repeat on the second side. Remove with a slotted spoon and reserve. Repeat in batches until all of the beef is browned.

Add the onions, celery, carrots, and leek to the Dutch oven. Season lightly with salt and pepper and stir to coat. Cook for 5 minutes, or until just softened. Add the garlic and tomato paste, stir to coat, and cook over medium-high heat for 2 minutes. Sprinkle the flour evenly over the mixture, stir to coat, and cook for 1 minute. Deglaze with the fresh orange juice, stir to pick up brown bits, and cook down to a glaze. Return reserved bacon, strained marinade liquid, and browned beef to the Dutch oven. Add the bay leaves, prunes, olives, herb bundle, lavender, and cognac or bourbon. Season lightly with salt and pepper. Bring to a boil over high heat, then reduce to a gentle simmer over low to medium-low heat. Cover and cook for $2\frac{1}{2}$ hours, skimming off any visible fat or foam along the way.

Remove cover and cook 1 hour more. Remove herb bundle and bay leaves. Increase heat to medium-high, and cook to reduce the sauce level until just below the surface of the beef and solid ingredients, about 15 minutes. Taste, and adjust seasonings. Stir in the fresh parsley and orange zest. Serve by itself or over warm rice.

CASSOULET

(MAKES 12 TO 14 SERVINGS)

Cassoulet *is a pretty word that sounds infinitely more fluttery and sexy than the sum of its humble meat and white bean parts. Replicating an authentic version stateside is difficult because beautiful charcuterie, duck legs, duck fat, and other key ingredients are harder to find. However, with a little smart shopping and ingenuity, it can be done. I use chicken thighs instead of duck confit, and find they break down beautifully into flavorful shreds, not unlike duck does in a more traditional cassoulet. This cassoulet is divided into two parts—a seasoned bean pot, and a tomato and meat stew; hence the need for two cooking pots.*

One of the most magical afternoons of my life was spent at my friend Maryse's rambling medieval home in Camon, situated in the heart of cassoulet country, the Languedoc Roussillon in south-central France. On that day she taught me how to make a real cassoulet. Her special techniques were slow cooking on an open, blazing hearth and repeatedly stirring the bread crust into the stew.

For the beans:

1 pound (2 1/2 cups) dry great Northern beans

15 cups water, divided

5 tablespoons olive oil

2 onions, coarsely chopped

2 carrots, peeled and coarsely chopped

5 large cloves garlic, smashed and coarsely chopped

Freshly ground black pepper

1 teaspoon dried thyme

1 teaspoon dried oregano

2 bay leaves

2 large smoked ham hocks (about 1 pound each)

Salt

For the tomato and meat stew:

4 slices bacon

2 1/2 pounds bone-in, skin-on chicken thighs, trimmed of excess fat

Salt and freshly ground black pepper

1 (1-pound) duck breast, cut into 4-6 pieces

14 ounces pork polska kielbasa, cut into 2-inch lengths

1 onion, diced medium

1 carrot, peeled and cut into a medium dice

5 large cloves garlic, smashed

1 1/2 cups crushed canned tomatoes

1 cup good-quality Chardonnay

2 cups Chicken Stock (see page 18)

2 bay leaves

6 sprigs fresh thyme, bundled with kitchen string

3 cups plain bread crumbs, preferably panko Japanese-style bread crumbs

1/4 cup reserved fat from browned meats

1 teaspoon dried thyme

Fresh thyme sprigs for garnish

Combine the dried beans and 6 cups water in a large glass bowl. Microwave on high for 3 minutes. Soak for a minimum of 3 hours, preferably overnight. Drain, rinse, and reserve.

Melt the olive oil over medium-high heat in the 8-quart Dutch oven. Add the onions, carrots, garlic, a generous pinch of pepper, thyme, and oregano. Stir to combine. Cook for 10 minutes, until softened and lightly browned. Add the drained, reserved beans, 8 cups water, bay leaves, and ham hocks. Bring to a boil over high heat, reduce to a simmer over medium-low, cover, and cook until the beans are tender, about 1 1/2 hours.

Remove the ham hocks. When cool enough to handle, cut off outer fat layer and cut the meat off the bones and into coarse chunks. Discard bones and fat, returning the meat to the bean pot. Remove the bay leaves. Add the remaining 1 cup water and season lightly with salt and pepper. Reserve contents in the pot.

For the tomato and meat stew, place the bacon in the 5 1/2-quart Dutch oven. Cook over medium-high heat, stirring once or twice, until the fat has been rendered, about 5 minutes. Remove the bacon with a slotted spoon and drain on paper towels. Reserve. Season the chicken thighs with salt and pepper. Brown the thighs skin side down in the rendered bacon fat until golden. Turn and brown the second side. Remove with a slotted spoon and reserve.

Drain off all but 3 tablespoons of the fat in the pan. Season the duck breast, and add to the Dutch oven skin side down; cook until golden and crisp, about 5 minutes. Turn and cook the other side. Remove with a slotted spoon and reserve with the other browned meats.

Pour off all but 3 tablespoons of the fat, reserving the fat separately. Add the kielbasa to the same Dutch oven and brown, stirring, for 5 minutes. Remove with slotted spoon and reserve with the other browned meats. Add the onion, carrot, and garlic to the pot, and season to taste with salt and pepper. Cook over medium heat until softened, about 5 minutes. Add the canned tomatoes and stir, then add the wine. Reduce by half over high heat. Chop the reserved bacon coarsely and return it along with the reserved chicken, duck, and sausage to the same pot. Add chicken stock, bay leaves, and thyme bundle. Cook covered over medium-low heat at a gentle simmer for 1 1/2 hours. Remove the bay leaves and thyme bundle.

To finish, preheat oven to 325 degrees F. Combine the tomato and meat stew with the cooked beans in the 8-quart Dutch oven, stirring to combine. Taste, and adjust seasoning as needed. Toss the bread crumbs with 1/4 cup of the reserved meat fats (save the rest for another use), salt and pepper to taste, and dried thyme. Distribute evenly over the top of the cassoulet. Cook uncovered for 1 hour. Reduce heat to 300 degrees F and cook for another 2 hours. Crush the crust that has formed with a wooden spoon, stirring it into the cassoulet. Increase heat to 500 degrees F and cook for another 15 minutes. Serve in bowls, and garnish with fresh thyme sprigs.

Daube d'Agneau au Curry et au Lait Du Noix de Coco
Curried Lamb and Coconut Milk Stew

(MAKES 8 TO 10 SERVINGS)

In Paris, I almost always stay at the same hotel in the 7th Arrondissement. Stunning views of La Tour Eiffel, Hotel Invalides, and Le Musée Rodin notwithstanding, another reason I stay there is the quaint little wife-and-husband-owned bistro just steps from the hotel. She flits about the tiny space with her pencil and pad, taking orders with a smile, while he turns out one delight after the next in the tiny kitchen. One of the best things on their always stellar menu is the curried lamb stew, which is commonly served at bistros throughout Paris. In my version of their delicious dish, slightly sweet coconut milk balances the heat of the red curry spice blend. Frozen peas, scallions, and parsley stirred in at the end make the dish pop with brilliant color in contrast to the reddish-brown hue of the decadent sauce.

2 tablespoons unsalted butter

2 tablespoons olive oil

4 pounds boneless leg of lamb, sinew removed, fat trimmed, and cut into 2-inch cubes

Salt and freshly ground black pepper

1 medium onion, finely chopped

4 cloves garlic, smashed and finely chopped

2 ribs celery, finely chopped

2 small carrots, peeled and finely chopped

2 cups coarsely chopped fresh tomatoes (skin-on, seed-in)

1 tablespoon red curry powder, more or less

1/2 teaspoon ground ginger

1/4 teaspoon crushed red pepper

1/2 cup freshly squeezed orange juice

2 tablespoons all-purpose flour

1 (13.66-ounce) can coconut milk (2 cups)

2 cups water

3/4 cup raisins

1/2 cup finely, diagonally sliced scallions

1/4 cup finely chopped fresh parsley leaves

2 cups frozen peas

3 tablespoons heavy cream

Hot cooked couscous or basmati rice

Melt the butter and olive oil in a 5 1/2-quart Dutch oven over medium-high heat. Meanwhile, season the lamb generously on all sides with salt and pepper. When the oil is just starting to sizzle, add half the lamb in a single layer; do not overcrowd. Cook until golden brown, about 5 minutes. Turn the lamb cubes and repeat on the second side. Remove with a slotted spoon and reserve. Repeat with the remaining lamb.

Reduce the heat to medium-low and stir in the onion, garlic, celery, and carrots. Season lightly

continued >

with salt and pepper. Toss to coat. Cook for 5 minutes, until just softened. Add the tomatoes, stir, and cook another 5 minutes. Stir in the curry, ginger, crushed red pepper, and orange juice. Increase heat to high and stir up any brown bits. Return the reserved lamb to the pot. Sprinkle in the flour, stir, and cook through for 1 minute. Add the coconut milk, water, and raisins. Bring to a boil over high heat, and then reduce to a low simmer, stirring occasionally. Cook for 2 hours and 15 minutes, or until the lamb is very tender and fragrant. (*Note*: Stop here if you like, cool off the stew, and refrigerate overnight. Do not add the remaining ingredients until just before serving.)

To finish, add scallions, parsley, peas, and cream. Heat through completely. Taste, and adjust seasonings as needed. Serve over couscous or basmati rice, prepared according to package directions.

ABOUT THE AUTHOR

Holly Herrick is a recipient of Le Grande Diplome in Pastry and Cuisine, Le Cordon Bleu, Paris, France. Fluent in French and a bonafide Francophile who once called Paris and southern France home, she now resides in Charleston, South Carolina. She is the author of seven cookbooks, including three in The French Cook series. A former restaurant critic and multi-awarded food and travel writer, she also enjoys tennis, swimming, farmers markets, and long walks around her adopted city. Follow her blogs and work at hollyherrick.com and charleston.thepermanenttourist.com.

Acknowledgments

I don't know the talented cooks who first created soup and stew delights such as French Onion Soup, Bœuf à la Bourguignonne, or Bouillabaisse, but I am taking this moment to personally thank them. I had more fun testing recipes and eating from this, my seventh cookbook, than any I can remember. I think these recipes are some of my best and were such joy to make, largely because of their time and practice-honed French method. Each one presented a fresh new memory of happy days spent in France. Thank you, beautiful France and wonderful French chefs!

My neighbor Lucie Maguire was indispensable to me on this book. She has always served as primary taster because she has an amazing palate and is brutally honest. Lucie and her soup-loving husband Bobby took front and center on this project, tasting and sipping soups almost every day and even sharing some with their brand new grandson, Scott. Thank you, Maguire family!

Huge gratitude goes to Doug Fox and Joey Blythe, market managers at the meat/seafood counter at my home away from home, the Harris Teeter grocery, downtown Charleston, South Carolina. Both avid gourmets and knowledgeable cooks, they generously shared tips on select cuts of meat and fish for various dishes, always with a smile and encouraging words. They help make food shopping a pleasure and an opportunity to learn.

Thank-you to super-talented photographer/stylist team Chia Chong and Libbie Summers for your beautiful work, wonderful attitudes, and professionalism. Thanks also to the production designer Melissa Dymock, at Gibbs Smith.

Writing a cookbook is a commitment, and some days go more smoothly than others. It helps having a support group. That small and special group is composed of my editor, Madge Baird, my darling friend and smile-maker Michael Keating, and my pets and frequent cooking companions, chocolate cocker spaniel Tann Mann and Chutney Cat. For them, I am deeply grateful.

INDEX

METRIC CONVERSION CHART

Volume Measurements	
U.S.	Metric
1 teaspoon	5 ml
1 tablespoon	15 ml
1/4 cup	60 ml
1/3 cup	75 ml
1/2 cup	125 ml
2/3 cup	150 ml
3/4 cup	175 ml
1 cup	250 ml

Weight Measurements	
U.S.	Metric
1/2 ounce	15 g
1 ounce	30 g
3 ounces	90 g
4 ounces	115 g
8 ounces	225 g
12 ounces	350 g
1 pound	450 g
2 1/4 pounds	1 kg

Temperature Conversion	
Fahrenheit	Celsius
250	120
300	150
325	160
350	180
375	190
400	200
425	220
450	230